THE SCIENCE OF
SOUND AND MUSIC

Shar Levine and Leslie Johnstone

Sterling Publishing Co., Inc.
New York

To Johnny Seguin—an inspirational music teacher, a brilliant drummer, and a great friend.—S.L.

To Alison Hunter, and the Pringles: Gary, Jennifer, Verity, and Allyn.—L.J.

Acknowledgments

We would like to express many thanks to Johnny Seguin for contributing his time, energy, and expertise. Thanks also to Dr. Pete Matthews, of the Department of Physics and Astronomy at the University of British Columbia, for his advice and guidance; and to Elana Brief for playing matchmaker.

For providing us with photographs, we are most grateful to the Vancouver Symphony Orchestra and Communications Manager Liz Parker; Katherine Calder-Becker of Lasido Inc.; Stan Garber of Selmer Instruments; the Vancouver Opera and Communications Manager Doug Tuck; the Vancouver Acquarium; David Gerhard; and Uzume Taiko.

Much gratitude, too, to: Jeff Connery for his terrific photos; and our models Alec, Dara, Dea, Janice, Jeffray, Jenn, and Robyn.

Editor: Danielle Truscott
Illustrator: Dave Winter
Photographer: Jeff Connery

Library of Congress Cataloging-in-Publication Data Available

10 9 8 7 6 5 4 3 2 1

Published by Sterling Publishing Company, Inc.
387 Park Avenue South, New York, N.Y. 10016
© 2000 by Shar Levine and Leslie Johnstone
Distributed in Canada by Sterling Publishing
C/o Canadian Manda Group, One Atlantic Avenue, Suite 105
Toronto, Ontario, Canada M6K 3E7
Distributed in Great Britain and Europe by Chris Lloyd
463 Ashley Road, Parkstone, Poole, Dorset, BH14 0AX, England
Distributed in Australia by Capricorn Link (Australia) Pty Ltd.
P.O. Box 6651, Baulkham Hills, Business Centre, NSW 2153, Australia
Printed in China

Sterling ISBN 0-8069-7183-5

Contents

Introduction   4
Note to Parents and Teachers   5
Safety First!   6
Materials   7

WHAT IS SOUND?   8

Clap Your Hand(s)!   9
Do the Wave   11
All Fall Down   13
Good Vibrations   15
Hey Pitcher, Pitcher!   17
Keep Your Ear to the Ground   19
Coming and Going   21
Hello, Hello   22
Put a Lid on It   24

MAKING SENSE OF SOUND   26

I'm All Ears   27
Beat of a Different Drummer   30
Where Are You?   32
Knot Hear!   33
Balancing Act   35
Direct Connection   36
Shake, Rattle, and Roll!   38
Say "Ah!"   40
Vocal "Chords"   42
Mystery Voices   44

MUSIC TO MY EARS   46

That Doggone Talent!   47
Stretched to the Limit   49

You Can Tune a Piano, but You Can't
    Tuna Fish   51
Spouting Bowl   53
Is It Live?   55
Timber!   58
Pick-Up Sticks   60

INSTRUMENTAL ACCOMPANIMENT   62

Band on the Run   63
Knock on Wood   65
Sticky Stuff   67
The Ringing of Bells   69
Rimshot   72
Rainsticks   74
"Canned" Music   75
Reed My Lips   77
Glossary   78
Index   80

Introduction

The phrase "It's music to my ears!" has probably never been exclaimed by the parent of a child who's just learning to play the violin. So what is it that makes music different from **noise**, and is there a science behind this?

While it may not be immediately obvious, there is a relationship between music and science. Musical **scales**, for example, are based on math. Physics can be used to explain why violins have that funny *f* carved into the wood, why guitars have strings that are different widths, and why, when you hear a heavy drumbeat, you seem to feel it in your chest.

Sound is all around us—there is no place on Earth without it. Even on top of the highest mountain, or at the bottom of the deepest sea, there is some sort of noise. You just can't get away from it! The only place where there is no sound is in outer space.

Because sound is in our lives at every moment, it's important to understand where it comes from, how it works, and how it affects us. This book contains simple, safe experiments that allow you to do just that, using mostly everyday materials found around your house. With

nothing fancier than a handful of items from your kitchen, desk drawer, or garage, you'll discover how sound travels through the air; why the way you hear things affects how you speak; why some people's singing can charm birds from the trees, while others' drives friends and family from the house!; and all sorts of fascinating facts about musical instruments and how they work. You don't need to know how to play a musical instrument to enjoy this book, and you won't need to buy an instrument either (although you

already own one—your voice!). For the few experiments that require using a musical instrument that you might not have yourself, you can rent one, borrow one from a friend, or see if you can do the experiment at school, and use instruments owned by the school. But you'll find that just by using your voice and your ears, you can discover some very interesting and unusual things about sound.

Once you've learned a bit more about how science, sound, and music are all related, you might want to find out more about musical instruments. If so, check out whether your school has instruments that your class can borrow to study and play. Or ask your teacher to arrange a field trip to a music store, where you can see these instruments at close range.

If you are interested in how certain unusual instruments sound—for example, a didgeri-doo (a wooden or bamboo "trumpet" used by Australian aboriginals) or a djembe (an African goblet-shaped wooden drum with a goatskin drum-head)—you can find some really interesting recordings on the Internet. Some websites offer sound files you can play or even download that will give you an idea of the kinds of music these exotic instruments make. When in doubt, you can check with your local library for more books and tapes on music, instruments, and science. Now get ready to solve some of the weird and wonder-ful mysteries of sound!

NOTE: Deaf people, or peo-ple who have difficulty hear-ing, may not be able to do all the experiments. But this book is designed so that at least half of the activities can be fully enjoyed by those whose hear-ing is not perfect. (If you're "tone deaf," or have trouble hearing the differences between pitches, you can still do all the experiments—but

take our advice and never try to serenade the love of your life with an out-of-tune guitar while singing in a completely different key! Just trust us on this one!)

NOTE TO PARENTS AND TEACHERS

NOTE TO PARENTS AND TEACHERS

As you know, children learn best when they are having a good time. This book gives you a great opportunity to combine science, math, and music while having fun with your kids or stu-dents. Forget about just telling them to practice their scales—instead, here's a way to teach them entertaining and unex-pected scientific facts about the sound around them!

In the classroom, there are many ways to inspire potential classical composers or aspiring rock 'n' rollers. You can start by organizing a trip to a music store, so that kids can see instru-

ments firsthand and maybe even try playing some. Many artists volunteer their time in schools and may be happy to perform for your class. Or ask your local high school band to play for your class one day.

One of the more fascinating aspects of music is watching an instrument being repaired. See if you and your child or your class can pay a visit to an instrument repair shop. Kids love watching a piano being tuned, a saxophone being taken apart, or even a guitar being re-strung, and doing so is a great opportunity for them to learn more about an instrument.

Another inexpensive and easy way to broaden children's musical horizons is to simply play a wide variety of types of music for them. You don't need to purchase new CDs; you can simply flip around to different radio stations and find different kinds of music. See if the kids can identify the instruments used in different recordings. If you're a teacher, ask your students to find pictures of various kinds of instruments and bring them to class. Start a home or classroom chart of "world instruments" that features music and instruments from around the globe!

Incorporating math into music is one more way to pump up the volume on learning. Have the kids count **beats** and learn about time signatures which behave like fractions. Or introduce simple physics concepts by allowing kids to pluck stretched rubber bands and discover the different sounds they can create.

Not every child will play an instrument and not every parent can afford music lessons or the price of the instrument. But a little detective work is likely to turn up talented, skilled music students at local high schools, colleges, and universities who will give inexpensive lessons, or possibly even volunteer their skills and time. (Be sure, of course, to thoroughly check his or her references before making any hiring decisions.)

Some studies have suggested that listening to classical music can raise intelligence. While there is no scientific proof of this, one thing is for certain: Listening to music can't hurt you unless you turn up the volume too loud. Now, get ready to help your child or students share in the joy of different kinds of music, and have fun with them finding the science hidden among the notes.

SAFETY FIRST!

DO'S

1. Do ask an adult before handling any materials, sharp tools, musical instruments, or equipment.

2. Do read all steps of any experiment and assemble your

equipment carefully, making sure you know what to do before you begin the experiment. Work on a stable surface where you have plenty of room.
3. Do tell an adult immediately if you hurt yourself in any way.

DON'TS

1. Don't turn up the volume really high on electronic equipment—you can damage both the equipment and your ears.

2. Don't put anything in your ears. Doing so can easily and seriously damage your hearing.
3. Don't touch any musical instrument or attempt to tune, play, or adjust it, unless an adult approves and supervises you.
4. Don't shout or make loud noises into anyone's ears.

MATERIALS

To complete all of the experiments in this book, you will need the following items. You probably already have most of them on hand. If not, borrow an item or two from a neighbor or friend, or make an inexpensive purchase. Happy gathering!

aluminum foil
aluminum rod
assorted musical instruments
balloon
bath towel
beans (dried)
bicycle
broomstick
buttons
cardboard box
cardboard sheets
cardboard tubes
card stock (lightweight)
cassette (blank)
cellophane tape
chairs (straight-backed)
chopsticks
containers (opaque) with lids
copper tubing
cork
crystal wine glass
dinner plate (with smooth surface)
door with doorknob
drinking glasses
electrical tape
eyedropper
facecloth
felt-tipped pens
fishing line
flashlight
flat baking pan
floor (wood, tile, or stone)
foam packing chips
food coloring
garden hose
glass bottles
glass jar with lid
hammer
hardcover book
leather scraps
lipsticks
marbles
masking tape

mattress
metal coat hangers
metal cooking pot
mirror
mixing bowl
modeling clay
pail with handle
paper
paper cups
pens
pencils
piece of wood
pillowcase
plastic bags
plastic pop bottles
playing card
popcorn (unpopped)
portable radio, cassette player, or CD
    player with earphones
reed or thick blade of grass
rice (uncooked)
rocks (small)
rope
rosin
rubber bands
ruler
sand
scarf (dark-colored)
scissors
spring (long) or Slinky®
steel wool
stool
straight pin
string (some thick, some thin)
sugar
table
tablespoon
tissue box
tissue paper
towel (large)
water
whistle
wood dowelling
wooden clothespin
wooden door
wooden spoon
wooden yardstick (meterstick)

WHAT IS SOUND?

Imagine that you are safely inside your house watching a storm outside. An immense bolt of lightning flashes across the sky, and several seconds later you hear a huge clap of thunder that shakes the house and rattles the windows. This is sound.

Sound is created when air is disturbed or moved—this movement or disturbance travels in **waves** from its source to our ears, giving us the sensation of hearing. Yet while we mostly think of sound as something we hear, we also feel sound sometimes. If you have ever been to a rock concert and stood close to the speakers, for example, you may have felt a thumping in your chest. This is the low-frequency sound of bass coming in waves from the speakers. In the case of thunder, the sound waves are sometimes large enough to vibrate objects around us.

Sound is around us all the time, and experiencing it is such an automatic part of our daily lives that most of us take it for granted. But when we take a minute to stop and think about it, we realize how important it is to our experience of the world. Because of sound, you can tell the difference between your mother's voice and a stranger's voice. You can distinguish the sound of a piano from that of a guitar. Without going outside or even looking out the window, you can tell whether it's raining outside or not.

In this section, you will learn about the physics of sound: what creates sound, how it travels through the air, how it is measured, and how we perceive it.

Clap Your Hand(s)!

Have you ever tried to clap using only one hand? Unless you hit your hand against another object—your leg, say, or a table—the action doesn't make a sound. On the other hand (if you'll pardon the pun), when you clap with both hands you can make a very loud sound. You can also alter the sound by changing the positions of your hands—by cupping your hands, or stretching your fingers backwards. When you clap with both hands, you *compress* the air, or push it together. Let's look at how this works!

WHAT YOU DO

1. Cover the top of the large mixing bowl with aluminum foil. Fold it tightly around the bowl's edges and smooth the surface of the foil.

2. Sprinkle the sugar in a thin layer on top of the foil.

3. Clap your hands above the sugar and watch what happens.

4. Try this again, this time banging a pot instead of clapping your hands. Hold the pot upside down above the foil-covered bowl and use a wooden spoon

WHAT YOU NEED

⚐ large mixing bowl smaller than 1 foot (30 cm) in diameter

⚐ 1-foot-square (30-cm-square) piece of aluminum foil

⚐ 1 teaspoon (5 ml) sugar

⚐ large metal cooking pot

⚐ wooden spoon

⚐ 1 teaspoon (5 ml) rice

Clapping your hands above the bowl makes the sugar react.

to bang the bottom of the pot. What happens to the sugar this time?

5. Blow or gently brush the sugar off the foil, then sprinkle rice in a thin layer on top of the foil and repeat steps 3 and 4. Does the rice move more than the sugar did ?

WHAT HAPPENED?

When you clapped your hands, you could hear the sound they made. This sound is caused by a **vibration** or movement created when your hands disturb the air. When you clapped, two things happened: you produced a noise and you moved air outwards. Air is made up of **molecules**, which are tiny particles too small to see. These molecules move around and allow sound vibrations to be passed along through the air to your ears. The vibrations also made the rice and sugar move slightly on the foil. The louder the sound is, the bigger the vibrations. Small particles like the sugar grains move more easily than larger particles like the grains of rice when exposed to the same amount of vibration. Another way to think of this is that when you moved the air molecules with your hands you gave them extra **energy**. This energy is also what caused the sugar and rice to move. Sound is a type of energy.

Bang the pot's bottom with a spoon and see what happens.

Clap your hands over the rice and it reacts differently.

Do the Wave

Have you ever been to a baseball game or another big event where people have done "the wave?" First one group of people stands up, then the group of people next to them stands and the first group of people sits. Several groups of people do this one immediately after another, and as the movement is repeated through the crowd it creates a ripple effect. Sound moves in much the same way as the people move. Particles of air or other materials are compressed or moved closer together. They hit the nearby particles and cause them to move closer together, and this passes along the material in a wave-like motion. Let's look at some different types of waves and how they happen.

settle until its surface is completely smooth and still.

3. Release a small drop of water from the eyedropper onto the surface of the water near the center of the pan. Watch what happens. Try this again, releasing several drops of water one after another.

WHAT YOU NEED

∾ shallow, flat, watertight pan or dish

∾ water

∾ eyedropper

∾ long spring or Slinky®

∾ helper

WHAT YOU DO

1. Place the shallow pan on a sturdy, level surface and fill it about halfway with water.

2. Draw up some of the water into an eyedropper. Allow the water in the pan to

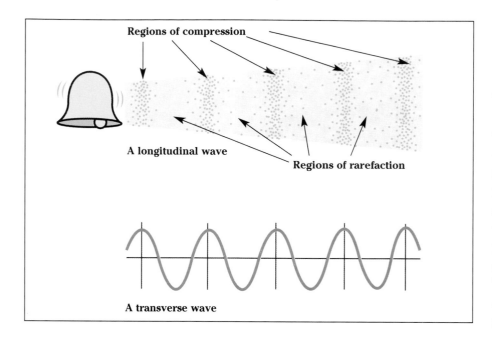

Regions of compression

A longitudinal wave

Regions of rarefaction

A transverse wave

move outward toward the sides of the container. When sound travels, it also moves outward from its source in all directions. To cause a sound, a vibrating object makes the molecules in the air around it move. The area of air where the particles are squeezed together is called a **region of compression.** As the sound moves, the area next to the region of compression has fewer air particles in it and is called a **region of rarefaction.** When you pushed and pulled on the end of the spring or Slinky, you saw the regions of compression and rarefaction move down the spring. This type of wave is called a **longitudinal** wave and is the type of wave sound makes when it travels through the air. The molecules in the air don't move very far when a sound wave passes through them, but the energy of the sound can move a long way. When you moved the spring or Slinky® from side to side, you could see a sideways ripple move down the spring. This type of wave is called a **transverse wave** and is the type of wave that occurs in the strings of instruments when they are plucked, bowed, or hammered.

4. Have a helper hold one end of the spring or Slinky® on the floor or a tabletop. Hold the other end of the spring firmly and move away from your helper so that the spring is stretched slightly and lying along the floor or table. Rapidly move your end of the spring toward your helper and away again, and watch what happens. Try moving the end of the spring several times, one time

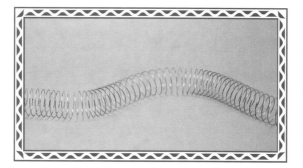

The Slinky® moves in a transverse wave.

right after the other. Watch what happens.

5. Next, instead of moving the end of the spring away from and toward your helper, try moving it rapidly from side to side. What happens now?

WHAT HAPPENED?

When the water drops hit the surface of the water, they caused ripples or waves to

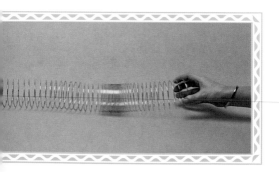

The Slinky® moves in a longitudinal wave.

All Fall Down

John Tyndall, a nineteenth-century Irish scientist, was our kind of guy. He loved to do large-scale demonstrations of physics principles. He once said, "Scientific education ought to teach us the invisible as well as the visible in nature; to picture with the eye of the mind those operations which entirely elude the eye of the body." In other words, in order to understand the way some things work in the world around us, it's sometimes very important to understand what you can't see. This next experiment is based on one Tyndall did in 1870 to show how sound travels through air. Just think of yourself as a human domino when you do this experiment.

WHAT YOU NEED

∾ 5 friends about the same size

∾ mattress or other soft surface

WHAT YOU DO

1. Have your friends stand one behind the other so they form a line, with the person in the front of the line facing the mattress or other soft surface. Each person should be a little less than an arm's length away from the person behind or in front of him or her.

2. Have everyone stand with his or her legs slightly apart and place their hands firmly against the back of the person in front of them.

Imagine your friends as molecules.

Molecules pushing against each other form a longitudinal wave.

Sound travels in much the same way as your "chain of friends" moves.

3. Gently push the last person in the line forward and watch what happens.

WHAT HAPPENED?

When you pushed the person standing last in line forward, he or she had to push against the person in front in order to keep from falling. This is a natural reflex. He or she remained standing because of this reflex action. The next person in front had to do the same thing, and so on down the line. The last person pushed had no one to push against and therefore fell forward on to the soft surface. This is a model of the way sound travels in longitudinal waves, when each air molecule is pushed by nearby molecules. The molecules don't move very far, but the sound can travel a long distance.

CHAIN REACTION

According to the *Guinness Book of World Records*, the greatest number of dominos ever toppled was 1,138,101 on January 2, 1988, by thirty students from Delft, Eindhoven, and Twente Technical Universities in the Netherlands. They managed to set this wave of over a million dominos in motion with only a single push! You sure wouldn't want to try this one using people instead of dominos!

Good Vibrations

When you hear a loud noise, you might cover you ears and say, "Oh! That hurts!" Well, it would make just as much sense if you said, "Oh, that *hertz*." Heinrich Hertz, a nineteenth-century German scientist, discovered radio waves, and the unit of measurement used to describe the **frequency** of sound waves—a **hertz (Hz)**—is named after him. Frequency is the number of waves that pass a certain point in a given amount of time. One hertz is the same thing as one wave passing a certain point in one second. Can you actually see these waves? Let's investigate.

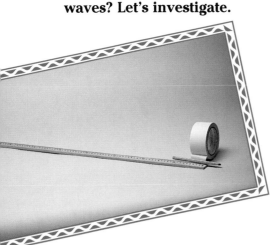

WHAT YOU NEED

- felt-tipped pen
- masking tape
- wooden yardstick (meterstick)
- hardcover book
- 8½ × 11-inch (22 × 28-cm) piece of lightweight card stock
- helper

WHAT YOU DO

1. Use the masking tape to attach the felt-tipped pen to one end of the wooden yardstick (or meterstick) so the pen extends about 1 inch (2.5 cm) past the end of the stick.

2. Place the yardstick flat on a table so that the end of the stick with the pen attached extends past the end of the table by 18 inches (45 cm). Have your helper place the book on top of the yardstick and press it down

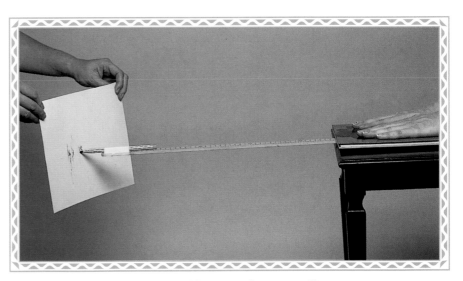

Push down on the ruler end and let go, and waves will appear.

so that the stick rests firmly on the tabletop.

3. Push down on the end of the yardstick with the pen attached, then let it go and allow it to vibrate. Listen to the sound it makes. While the stick is still vibrating, hold the card stock and move it horizontally and straight along the pen's tip so that as the pen moves up and down, it makes wavy lines on the card.

4. With your helper, reposition the book and ruler with pen attached so the pen end of the ruler extends 20 inches (50 cm) past the end of the table, and repeat step 3.

WHAT HAPPENED?

When you pushed down on the end of the ruler and let go, the end of the ruler moved up and down; when the pen moved up and down and you moved the card stock against it, a wave pattern appeared on the card. When the ruler section sticking out was longer, the vibration was greater and slower, and the wave pattern that appeared on the card stock was different. If you pulled the card across the end of the pen at exactly the same speed in step 4 as you did in step 3, you had fewer waves on the card.

Scientists use a device called an **oscilloscope** to look at sound waves. This device is connected to a microphone.

Sounds cause the diaphragm inside the microphone to vibrate, and an electrical signal is sent to the oscilloscope, where waves appear on its screen. The waves look a little like the transverse waves you created and learned about in the "Do the Wave" experiment (see page 11). The oscilloscope allows scientists to examine and measure sound waves.

ANIMALS AND HEARING

Normally, human beings can hear sounds with frequencies between about 20 Hz and about 20,000 Hz. The lower frequencies are sounds that have a lower pitch or deeper sound. The higher frequencies have a higher sound or pitch. Some animals can hear a much greater range of sounds. If you have a dog, you may have noticed that it can hear sounds you can't. Dog whistles don't seem to make any sound at all, yet dogs still hear them. Here are the hearing ranges of some animals that have been tested:

Bat	1,000 to 210,000 Hz
Cat	60 to 65,000 Hz
Dog	15 to 50,000 Hz
Dolphin	150 to 200,000 Hz
Elephant	5 to 18,000 Hz
Frog	50 to 10,000 Hz
Human	20 to 20,000 Hz
Pigeon	0.1 to 15,000 Hz

An oscilloscope measures sound waves.

The waves are different depending on the sound being measured.

Hey Pitcher, Pitcher!

Baseball might be the first thing that comes to mind when you hear the word **"pitch."** But pitch is also a very important part of sound. Pitch can be used to describe a number of things. If you were to arrange musical sounds from the lowest to the highest you can still hear, you would be ordering the sounds according to their pitch. Most people can tell which note is higher or lower when they hear it. Some people have what is called "absolute pitch," or perfect pitch, which means they can actually identify which note they are hearing. Here's a way of looking at frequency and seeing what effect it has on pitch.

WHAT YOU NEED

↬ bicycle

↬ playing card

↬ wooden clothespin

Warning: *Do not put your fingers into the spokes of the bicycle while its wheels are turning.*

WHAT YOU DO

1. Turn the bicycle upside down, so that its seat and handlebars rest on the floor. Make sure its position is stable, so that it won't fall over while you are doing the experiment.

2. Position the playing card on

the frame of the bicycle and use the clothespin to secure the card to the frame so that when the bicycle's wheel spins, the spokes will hit the card.

3. Use your hand to gently rotate the bicycle's pedals so that the bike's wheels turn slowly. Listen to the sound the card makes against the spokes.

4. This time, rotate the pedals a little faster and listen to the sound the card makes as the wheels turn more quickly than before. Is the sound higher or lower?

Use the clothespin to firmly secure the card to the bike's frame.

WHAT HAPPENED?

The sound was different depending on how slowly or fast you pedaled. When you pedaled slowly, the card moving against the spokes produced a tapping sound. When you made the wheel turn so that the card hit the spokes at least twenty times per second, you heard a very low-pitched sound. As you increased the speed, the sound got higher, or was at a higher pitch. Not all sounds can give you a sense of pitch. Only periodic, or off-and-on, sounds can give you that sensation. In order to tell a difference in pitch, you need to hear two sounds or notes that you can compare to each other.

Pure notes, or notes at a single frequency, can be created by an electronic device called an **oscillator**, which is attached to an amplifier and a loudspeaker. If you use a tuning fork, a special pronged metal device that you strike to make a sound, you can also hear an almost pure tone. In "Good Vibrations" (see page 15), you learned that humans can hear roughly from 20 Hz to 20,000 Hz. People can't identify sounds above or below this range.

ULTRASOUND AND INFRASOUND

Sound that is too high in pitch for humans to hear is called ultrasound. You may have even had your picture taken with ultrasound without knowing it! Huh?

Here's how it works: Doctors use ultrasound equipment to show an image of a foetus while it is still inside the mother's body. This equipment sends out waves that go into the mother's body and are reflected as they hit the foetus. The machine uses this information to create a picture of the foetus on a screen. Doctors also sometimes use ultrasound to look at the internal organs of your body. Sonar (Sound Navigation and Ranging), an underwater detection system used by ships and submarines, also uses ultrasound. Bursts of ultrasound are sent out into the water and the reflected sound gives a picture of the ocean floor. Sonar is so sensitive it can even be used to tell the size of a school of fish. Sounds too *low* in pitch for humans to hear are called infrasound. Just because you can't hear infrasound doesn't mean it can't affect you. In fact, the low-frequency sounds produced by some types of machinery can cause your body to vibrate and result in internal bruising and even death. Some researchers think that the infrasound produced by cars may be one of the causes of carsickness.

Keep Your Ear to the Ground

If you've ever watched an old Wild West movie, you've probably seen a character bending over with his head to the ground, listening for the sound of horses. Do you think he can tell how close the horses are? Or, if you've watched an old comedy, maybe you've seen a character with one end of a glass to his or her ear and the other end pressed to the wall, trying to eavesdrop on people in the next room. Do you think he or she can hear what they're saying? You know that sound travels through air. But can it also travel through other materials, like the ground or walls? Try this and see!

WHAT YOU NEED

~ radio or cassette player and music cassette, or portable CD player and CD

~ earphones

~ small towel or facecloth

~ wooden door

~ drinking glass

~ glass window

~ helper

~ wooden table

WHAT YOU DO

1. Attach the earphones to the CD or cassette player. Put on the earphones and play music at a level that is comfortable to listen to. Turn off the player, but do not change the settings.

2. Wrap the small towel around one earphone so that music can only be heard from the other earphone.

3. Have your helper stand on one side of a closed door while you stand on the other side. Have him or her first turn on the portable player on his or her side of the closed door. Then place the earphone directly on the door. Put your ear to your side of the door and see if you can hear the music. Try this again, this time using a drinking glass to listen. The open end of the glass should be against the door and the bottom of the glass against your ear. How does this affect the sound of the music? Try turning the glass so the closed end is

First, listen with your naked ear to music through the door.

19

against the door and the open end is against your ear. Is the noise louder or softer this way?

4. Have your helper hold the earphone against the glass of a window, and place your ear on the other side of the window. Can you hear the sound through the glass?

5. This time, have your helper put the earphone on top of a wooden table. Stand at the opposite end of the table with your ear to the table. Can you hear the music? Try moving the earphone along the tabletop toward you. Does the distance make any difference in terms of how you hear the sound?

WHAT HAPPENED?

You were able to hear the sound more easily when it traveled through the wood or the glass than when it traveled through the air. Why? Remember: Sound travels in waves through the different materials. Because the molecules, or particles, in air are quite far apart, sound travels quite slowly through air; the molecules in air also move around, so the sound's vibration can be changed or lost. In solid materials like the wood of the table or the window glass, the particles are more tightly bound together, and so the sound goes faster. The closer you are to the source of sound—the more quickly it reaches you—the louder the sound will be.

Listen again, using a glass.

THE SPEED OF SOUND

The speed of sound in the air is measured at sea level at 32°F (0°C). At that temperature and pressure, sound travels at 1,088 feet (332 meters) per second. Sound travels faster through materials that are made up of particles more tightly bound together. The chart at right gives you some idea of how the speed of sound changes when it travels through different kinds of materials.

Sound travels through:

~ Fresh water (77°F or 25° C) at 4,893 ft/s (1493 m/s)

~ Brick at 11,980 ft/s (3,650 m/s)

~ Wood (oak) at 12,617 ft/s (3850 m/s)

~ Glass at 14,900 ft/s (4,540 m/s)

~ Steel at 17,100 ft/s (5,200 m/s)

Is it true that if you scream in outer space, no one can hear you? In a word, yes. Sound can't travel through a **vacuum**, or empty space. This is because there are no air molecules for it to push around. Sound can only travel through a medium—air, water, or some other material.

Coming and Going

Have you ever noticed that when a fire engine, ambulance, or police car goes by with its lights and sirens blaring, the sound seems to change as the vehicle passes you? In 1842, a scientist named Dr. Christian Johann Doppler discovered why sound moves from a higher note to a lower note as the vehicle passes by. The cause of this movement of sound was named after him, and is called the **Doppler effect.** In fact, the siren keeps making the same sound—you just hear it differently. Let's take a peek at how this works.

WHAT YOU NEED

➤ clean 4-foot-long (1.2 meter) piece of garden hose

WHAT YOU DO

1. Sing the sound "tooooooooo."
2. Use one hand to hold the hose at one of its ends. Put the opening of the hose against your mouth. Place your other hand on the hose at your waist level. Sing the sound you practiced in step 1 into the hose, and use your lower hand to twirl the loose end of the hose in a large circle. Listen to the changing sound.

WHAT HAPPENED?

When you twirled the loose end of the hose, the sound seemed to become higher and lower, higher and lower. The higher sound was caused by sound waves being pushed together as the end of the hose approached your ear—the **wavelength** was shortened and the frequency of the waves was increased. When the frequency of sound waves increases, this makes the sound higher, or gives the sound a higher pitch. When the end of the hose moved away from you, the sound waves moved further apart; the wavelength increased and the frequency decreased. Sounds at a lower frequency have a lower pitch.

The sounds' pitches depend on how far or near the hose end is to your ear.

THE DOPPLER EFFECT

Police use the Doppler effect to catch speeding drivers. Radio waves are sent out from radar guns, and the waves bounce off of passing cars. The waves bounce back to a detector that measures their frequency. If the car approaching the detector is speeding, the waves bounced back to the detector will be closer together than if the car is traveling at the posted legal speed. This change in the frequency of sound as the source of sound moves toward or away from an observer is called the Doppler effect.

Hello, Hello

If you've ever stood in a canyon, you may have heard the **echo** of your own or someone else's voice. The sound of a voice can be reflected back to you by a natural rock formation. But did you know there are animals that use the reflection of sound to find things? Bats and dolphins are two creatures that use a process called **echolocation.** Dolphins send out short pulses of sound at a really high-pitched range, somewhere around 200,000 Hz. They can send out anywhere between ten to 200 pulses per second. As these sound waves go out, they hit various objects, such as fish. As the waves hit the fish, they send back a "sound picture" of the creatures and let the dolphin know if it is in danger, or if there's food close by. In a similar way, a bat's high-pitched squeaks bounce off solid objects, allowing the bat to navigate and avoid bumping into things as it flies around. Bats have special ears that have a unique muscle inside. This muscle acts like a switch, allowing the bat to turn off its hearing when it sends out a shriek, and turn on its hearing to hear the echo of the noise. So how do these echoes happen? Here's one way to find out.

WHAT YOU NEED

~ 2 large mailing tubes, several feet (a meter or so) long

~ large, smooth dinner plate

~ bath towel

~ cassette or CD player with earphones

~ small towel or facecloth

~ table

~ helper

WHAT YOU DO

1. Place the tubes on the table at a 45° angle to each other. Have your helper hold the plate upright with the front facing the tubes, several inches away from the point at which the two tubes meet.
2. Cover one earphone attached to the cassette or CD player with the small towel or facecloth. Put the other earphone into the end of one of the tubes facing the plate. Turn on the cassette or CD player.
3. Put your ear to the end of the open tube that's farthest away from the plate. Can you hear the music from the player?
4. Have your helper remove the plate and put a folded bath towel in its place. Try the experiment again. Can you still hear the music?

WHAT HAPPENED?

When the plate was positioned at the end of the angled tubes,

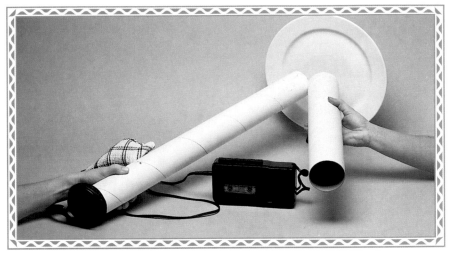

Sound waves bounce off a smooth surface.

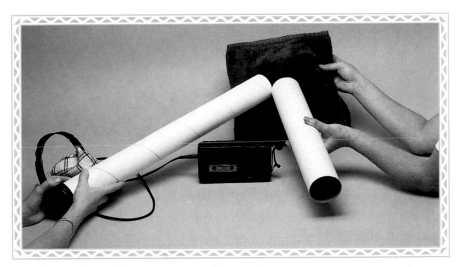

Rougher surfaces, like a towel, absorb sound waves.

you could hear the music, but when the towel was there, you couldn't hear anything. Why? Because the plate's smooth surface allowed the sound waves to bounce, or reflect, off of it, and direct the waves down the second tube. Sound waves can change direction. When a sound wave hits a smooth, hard surface, it can be reflected, or bounced off of the surface, just like light off of a mirror. The towel is rough and full of tiny air pockets that absorbed the waves, which is why you couldn't hear the music. Echoes are caused by sounds bouncing back and forth so that it seems as if there are several repetitions of the same sound.

WHISPERING WALLS

Did you know that there are buildings that use the reflection of sound to produce interesting effects? One such building is in London, England. A room called the "Whispering Gallery" in Saint Paul's Cathedral was designed and constructed between 1675 and 1710 by Sir Christopher Wren. When you stand on one side of the rounded room, you can whisper and be clearly heard by someone on the other side of the building. Another such wall is located in Beijing, China, at the Winter Palace. Some science museums also have modern-day examples of "whispering" rooms that look like giant satellite dishes. As you speak into one, a friend can hear you from hundreds of feet away.

Put A Lid on It

Sometimes loud sounds get to be just *too* loud. When that happens, there are a few things that you can do (apart from calling the police to shut down the party!). One simple solution is to use earplugs. Or you can dull or "muffle" the sound with some kind of padding material. Drummers sometimes put blankets inside their bass drums to muffle the sound so that you can clearly hear the other instruments. Some materials work better as mufflers than others. Try this experiment to see which ones work the best.

WHAT YOU NEED

- radio, or cassette or CD player
- cardboard box larger than the radio or cassette or CD player
- tissue paper
- plastic bags
- pillowcase
- large towel
- foam packing chips
- aluminum foil

WHAT YOU DO

1. Turn on the radio, or cassette or CD player, and adjust the volume so that you can hear music when the radio is placed into the cardboard box and the lid of the box is closed.

2. Open the box and surround the radio with the tissue paper. Close the lid of the box and listen to see if you can hear the music.

3. Open the box and remove the tissue paper. (Don't leave the radio on for too long as it may overheat.) Now loosely crumple the plastic bags and arrange them around the radio as you did with the tissue in step 2. Close the box again, and see how the music sounds now.

4. Repeat step 3, alternately using the pillowcase, large towel, foam packing chips, and aluminum foil, until you have tested all of the different materials.

WHAT HAPPENED?

The fuzzier materials, like the towel, muffled the sound the most because there are more tiny air holes in these materials that trap the sound. Thicker layers of material also act as more effective mufflers.

Architects, or people who design buildings, use the science of **acoustics** when they are designing large spaces such as concert halls. Acoustics deals with how sound is produced, controlled, transmitted, and received. Sometimes, for example, architects make use of the muffling effects of different materials when they design concert halls. When a large space like an auditorium has smooth walls, sound will often begin to bounce around and cause echoes, making it difficult to

Start with a radio and a simple cardboard box.

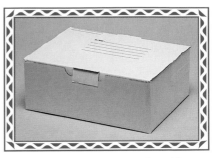

Make sure the radio can fit with some room inside the closed box.

How you hear the music may change when you add tissue paper.

Wrap the radio in a towel and see if the sound is quieter or louder.

When you surround the radio with foil, the sound is louder again.

Foam packing chips have another effect on the sound's volume.

hear the music the way it is supposed to be heard. To avoid this problem, architects use several different devices. They add ornamentation to the walls in the form of small designs or sculptures, which breaks up the smooth surface and reduces the echoing. Acoustic tiles with hundreds of tiny holes that absorb sound are often attached to the

ceilings or walls of concert halls. Often, chandeliers or other large, specially devised structures are suspended from the ceiling to absorb and scatter sound. Even audiences affect the echoing of halls: the more people there are in an audience, and the heavier the clothing they wear, the more sound will be absorbed.

MAKING SENSE OF SOUND

This section deals with sound as it relates to your hearing and some of your other senses. You learned to speak at such a young age that there's a good chance you don't remember it, and you definitely don't remember learning to hear. Why's that? Because when babies are born, they already know how to hear. In fact, many parents talk to them before they are even born—some expectant parents play classical music or read out loud when the mother is pregnant, because they believe that it will make their babies smarter. Hearing and speaking are directly related: for example, babies who can't hear often have difficulty learning how to speak.

You might like to listen to music with the volume turned up quite high, and although your parents might think you just do it to annoy them (and this might be true sometimes!), there is also a scientific reason that may explain why you like to do this. When music is played loudly, its sound becomes richer in tone, and as a result your ears and hearing become more sensitive to the lows and highs. Unfortunately, listening to very loud music damages your ears and hearing, and despite the modern advances with hearing aids, once your hearing has been damaged, it can't be repaired. Considering this, and the fact that older people sometimes begin to lose their ability to hear as part of the aging process, it's very important to protect your hearing now. Doing so may allow you to be able to hear well all your life. If you're listening to music and you get a headache, or if your ears start to ring, this is an indication that a noise is too loud and it is hurting your ears. So turn down the volume.

For some people, sound is connected to a sense you probably don't think of it s being linked to—sight. People who have a condition called **synesthesia** experience sounds by seeing them as colors. Different sounds sometimes remind all of us of different colors,

though. In tests where students were asked to relate color to music, it was found that high-pitched notes made people think of bright colors , while low tones called to mind dark colors. White, yellow, and pink were associated with tones in the 4,000-Hz range; blue and green were associated with tones in the 1,000-Hz range; and brown, gray, and black were associated with tones in the 200-Hz range. Students also thought of the "moods" of different kinds of music, or different sounds, in terms of colors: red represented lively music; blue, romantic or tender music; black, sad music. What color do you see when you listen to your favorite song?

Those of us who don't experience colors with sounds often have other kinds of responses. The sound of a giggle can make you laugh, and loud crashing noises can make you jump. You can make a lot of different sounds with your own personal instrument, your voice. In this section you will learn how your ears, nose, and throat work together to create a human musical instrument.

I'm All Ears

You've probably heard the old saying, "It was so quiet you could hear a pin drop," but have you ever *actually* heard a pin drop? Considering how little noise a pin hitting a floor makes, it's pretty amazing that you can hear it. Your ears are amazing things. They collect the sounds you hear, then change the sound vibrations into nerve impulses that travel to your brain, where you interpret the impulses as sounds. You can detect subtle differences, such as which of your friends is calling you on the phone, with ease. Even in a noisy room, you can pick out someone saying your name. In this activity, you will improve your ability to hear, and look at exactly how all of this works.

WHAT YOU NEED

∾ 8 ½ × 11-inch (22 × 27.5-cm) piece of light cardboard

∾ masking tape

∾ helper

∾ table

∾ pin

∾ 12-inch (30-cm) ruler

Warning: *Never stick anything other than your fingers or earplugs into your ears; even these should be done while you are supervised by an adult.*

WHAT YOU DO

1. Bend the cardboard so that it forms a cone shape with a small opening at one end. Tape the cone together with masking tape.

2. Put your ear to the surface of the table at one end. At the other end of the table, have your helper hold a pin 10 inches (25 cm) above the surface and drop the pin onto the table. Make sure that you can hear the pin drop. If you need to, move a little closer to your helper. Mark the position of your ear on the table with a small piece of tape.

3. Place the small end of the cardboard cone near your ear. Move the open end of the cone to the tape on the table near where your helper dropped the pin.

4. Have your helper hold the pin 10 inches (25 cm) above the surface of the table and drop the pin again.

Position yourself so that when your helper drops the pin, you can hear it.

Listening with the cardboard cone alters your perception of sound.

WHAT HAPPENED?

When you used the cardboard cone to listen to the pin drop, the sound was louder than when you listened without the cone. The cone directed more of the sound waves coming from the pin toward your ear. This is the same way your **outer ear** directs the sound into your ear.

PARTS OF THE EAR

We usually talk about the parts of the ear as if the ear were divided into three parts. The external or **outer ear** is made up of two parts: the **pinna**, which is the funnel-shaped part where earrings are attached, and the tube-like **auditory canal**. The pinna acts like the cone you made in the "I'm All Ears" experiment you just did, directing sounds into the ear. The auditory canal is a tube about 1 inch (2.5 cm) long that the sounds travel through to reach the **tympanic** membrane, or eardrum, in the **middle ear**. The eardrum is a thin **membrane** that vibrates when hit with sound vibrations, just like the cookie sheet did in the "Clap Your Hand(s)!" experiment (see page 19); it has hairs and wax in it to protect your ears from dirt and dust. Resting against the eardrum on the inner side are tiny ear bones. The first bone is called the **malleus** or "hammer" bone: it rests directly against the eardrum and is attached to the next bone, the **incus**, or "anvil". The anvil is attached to the **stapes**, or "stirrup" bone, which rests against the **cochlea**. (Here's a piece of information that may come in handy if you're ever in a trivia contest: The stapes is the smallest bone in your body!) The malleus, incus, and stapes bones work together to transmit and increase sound vibration to the **inner ear** so that it can be heard. The cochlea is tiny, only about the size of a pea. It is a long tube, coiled up like a snail's shell. Inside the tube there is fluid, and attached to the inside are about 15,000 tiny hairs of different lengths. When different sound vibrations pass into the cochlea, they cause different hairs to vibrate. This information passes to the brain through the **auditory nerve**, which is attached to the cochlea. Your brain interprets the nerve messages as a specific sound. The **semicircular canals**, three tube-like structures that are used for balance, are also part of the inner ear (see "Balancing Act," page 35).

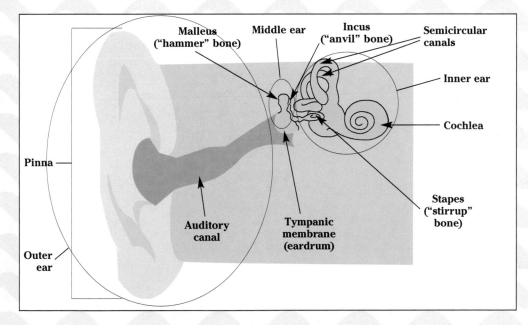

Malleus ("hammer" bone) · Middle ear · Incus ("anvil" bone) · Semicircular canals · Inner ear · Cochlea · Stapes ("stirrup" bone) · Tympanic membrane (eardrum) · Auditory canal · Pinna · Outer ear

Beat of a Different Drummer

When a doctor takes a funny-looking flashlight and looks inside your ears, what do you think he or she sees? Though it might seem like it, the doctor is not looking at your brains! He or she is looking inside your ears to see some of the various working parts. If you haven't been cleaning your ears regularly, you might have enough wax in there to make a candle, and that could be a problem! If your eardrum is throbbing and colored bright red, that could also be a problem—you could have an ear infection. Fortunately, most of the time our ears look just the way they are supposed to, but just how do they work? Let's take a look.

WHAT YOU NEED

- large balloon
- wide cardboard tube
- rubber band
- scissors
- 1 square inch (2.5 cm × 2.5 cm) of aluminum foil
- cellophane tape
- flashlight
- helper

WHAT YOU DO

1. Inflate the balloon. With one hand, hold one open end of the cardboard tube against your mouth. Use the other hand to hold the inflated balloon against the other open end of the tube. Speak into the tube. How does the balloon feel?

2. Now you get to make a very loud noise. Take the scissors and cut the tied end of the balloon so the air goes out of it. You will be left with an opened, stretched rubber balloon.

3. Stretch the balloon over the end of the cardboard. Use a rubber band to hold the balloon stretched in place over one open end of the tube.

4. Roll a piece of tape into a ring, with the sticky side out. Attach the foil to the ring and place the other end of the sticky ring into the center of the balloon.

5. Have your helper shine a light on the aluminum foil square, so that it reflects on a wall. Make different sounds into the tube and watch the reflection.

Feel the balloon's reaction when you speak into the tube.

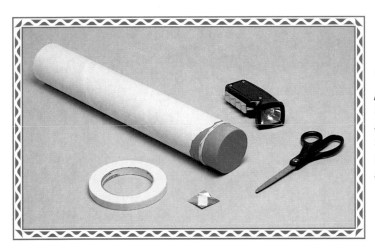

When the popped balloon is secured on the tube, add the foil square.

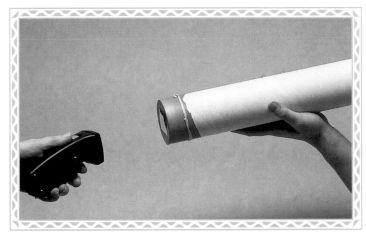

Your voice in the tube affects reflections made by the flashlight shining on the foil.

WHAT HAPPENED?

You created a working model of your tympanic membrane, or eardrum. Your eardrum is a thin membrane that is stretched across the end of the auditory canal in your ear. When you made a noise in the tube in step 1, you caused the vibration to move down the tube, which then vibrated on the balloon. The auditory canal acts in the same way as the tube, directing the vibration on to your eardrum. The vibrations you felt were caused by the sound waves from your voice. When you made different noises into the tube in step 5, you also made the surface of the balloon vibrate. This moved the piece of foil. You could see the effect of different sounds by observing the reflection of the light on the wall. The malleus, or hammer bone, in your middle ear is set in motion by the vibration of the eardrum in much the same way as the foil. Your doctor may be able to see the end of this bone as a dark spot where it touches your eardrum.

Where Are You?

If someone asked you whether you have a good "binauricular audition" system in your home that gives you great "auditive perspective," you might not have any idea what he or she meant. But the fancy words were the first ones used to describe stereo recording and its effects, when stereo was introduced at the Electrical Exhibition in Paris in 1881. In plain English, they mean that music is sometimes recorded in stereo, which means that when you listen to it, you hear different sounds in each ear. Stereo sound requires two speakers with different sounds coming from each, and makes sound that is recorded sound more like it's live. Here's a simple experiment to help you understand how it works.

WHAT YOU NEED

- stool
- helper
- dark scarf
- radio

WHAT YOU DO

1. Sit on the stool and have your helper blindfold you.
2. Have your helper stand in different places around the room and make a noise by snapping his or her fingers or clapping. Have him or her try snapping or clapping above your head, behind your back, next to your ears, and in other locations. See if you can tell where the noise is coming from.

3. Cover one ear with your hand and repeat step 2. Can you still tell where the noise is coming from?

4. This time, turn on the radio and repeat step 2. Have your helper make the same noises. Is it harder to tell where the noise is coming from now?

5. Trade places. Can your helper tell where the noises are coming from?

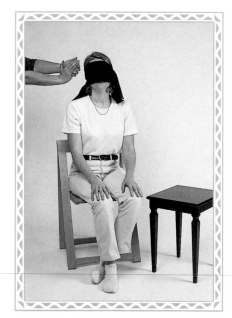

Start by listening to your helper clap his or her hands in different parts of the room.

WHAT HAPPENED?

You could tell where the sound was coming from when you listened with both ears because

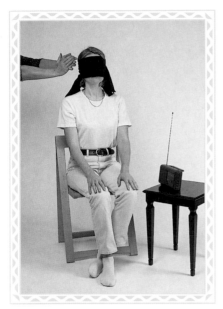

The more noises you listen to at once, the harder it is to distinguish sounds' sources.

you have something called **binaural hearing**. Simply put, this means that you have two ears! The difference in the sounds you hear in each ear is something that lets you know which direction the sound you're hearing is coming from. In part, you can determine the sound's direction because the ear that is closer to the source of the sound hears the sound more loudly than the ear that is farther away. There is also a very slight difference in timing—the nearer ear hears the sound first. It was harder to tell where the sound came from when you had one ear covered. The more noise there was in the room, the more difficult it was to find the source of the sound because the other sounds distracted you. When your helper snapped his or her fingers or clapped close to your ears, it was easier to tell where the sound was coming from.

Many kinds of animals, such as rabbits and horses, can move their outer ears in order to tell what direction sound is coming from. Owls are one of the few creatures with lopsided ears; their left ears are usually positioned higher on their heads than their right ears. This allows them to find the direction of even very faint sounds. Dogs have seventeen muscles attached to each of their ears. These muscles allow the dog to turn its ears, and also to raise and lower the ears slightly. Human beings, on the other hand, have only nine muscles attached to each ear, and they aren't used for very much unless you happen to be one of those talented people who can wiggle their ears.

Knot Hear!

You probably haven't asked yourself this question before, but which do you think is easier to fool—your ears or your brain? As you saw in the previous experiment, "Where Are You?", your ears can tell which direction a noise is coming from. Your ears take in the sound, and your brain does some sophisticated stuff and turns it into something you understand. Can you fake out your brain about what it's hearing?

WHAT YOU NEED

- ~ 2 large plastic pop bottles
- ~ scissors
- ~ two 3-foot-long (90-cm) pieces of rubber hose
- ~ electrical tape
- ~ 2 cone-shaped paper cups
- ~ wooden yardstick (meterstick) or long, thin piece of wood
- ~ adult helper
- ~ whistle

WHAT YOU DO

1. Have an adult measure about halfway down each of the pop bottles and cut each in half. Discard the bottom halves of the bottles. You'll use the two top halves as funnels.

2. Attach the bottleneck end of one of the funnels to one end of one piece of garden hose. Do the same with the second funnel and hose. If your funnels will not stay in place, use electrical tape to secure them.

3. Cut off the pointed ends of the paper cups to create a small funnel. Attach the bottom end of each paper cup to the free end of each hose.

4. Tape the hoses onto the yardstick in opposite directions, so that one funnel is at the 1-inch mark and the other funnel is at the 36-inch (90-cm) mark.

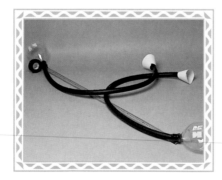

5. Place the open end of the cup attached to one funnel against your right ear, and the open end of the other cup against your left ear.

6. Have your helper move around you, snapping his or her fingers or clapping. Where do the sounds seem to come from? Now close your eyes and listen to the noises your helper is making.

WHAT HAPPENED?

The sounds probably seemed very strange to you. When you listened with your eyes open, you could see that your helper was on your left, but the sounds seemed to come from your right. When your helper was on your right, the sounds seemed to come from the left. How does that happen? Your brain has learned to interpret nerve impulses from your sensory organs such as your eyes and ears. When the information coming from these organs doesn't match up, it makes you feel disoriented. When you closed your eyes, the sounds seemed to make more sense, but you were still hearing the sounds in the "wrong" ears.

Balancing Act

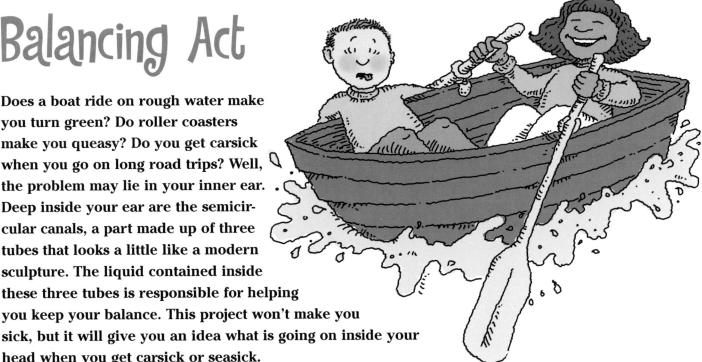

Does a boat ride on rough water make you turn green? Do roller coasters make you queasy? Do you get carsick when you go on long road trips? Well, the problem may lie in your inner ear. Deep inside your ear are the semicircular canals, a part made up of three tubes that looks a little like a modern sculpture. The liquid contained inside these three tubes is responsible for helping you keep your balance. This project won't make you sick, but it will give you an idea what is going on inside your head when you get carsick or seasick.

WHAT YOU NEED

➤ clear glass jar with lid
➤ water
➤ food coloring
➤ modeling clay

WHAT YOU DO

1. Fill the jar about halfway with water. Add a few drops of food coloring to the jar, and close the lid tightly.

2. Hold the jar so that it is vertical, or straight up and down, and observe the level of the water.

3. Prop the jar up at different angles using a small ball of modeling clay, or slowly turn the jar in different directions while watching the level of the water each time you move the jar.

The level of water inside the jar remains the same despite the jar's angle.

WHAT HAPPENED?

Each time you changed the position of the jar, the water stayed level, which is what happens inside your ear when you move around. The liquid in your ear slops around until it settles at a flat level. This helps you keep your balance. When you are moving fast and changing directions, like when you are on a ride in an amusement park, the liquid in your ears keeps swirling around in different directions. The liquid is inside the three tubes of the semicircular canals. One tube detects changes in the liquid level as you move vertically, or up and down; one detects forward motion; and the last tube detects horizontal, or side-to-side, motion. If the levels of the fluids in these tubes change too quickly, or if information the tubes detect is different that what your eyes are seeing, your brain gets confused and your stomach gets upset. Not a good combination! Some people who get motion sickness very easily have to take special medicines to prevent them from feeling rotten whenever they ride in a car, train, boat, or airplane. Luckily, there are a couple of ways to avoid getting motion sickness. You can:

Keep your eyes on the horizon—the line in the landscape where the earth or sea meets the sky—and don't look up and down.

Make sure that if you're spinning, either while you're on a ride or if you're playing or dancing, you don't turn your body and head at the same time. Turn your body, then your head. Keep your eyes focused on one point in the turn. This is a method ballet dancers use.

Direct Connection

When you don't want to listen to your parents or your baby brother or sister, do you stick your fingers in your ears to keep out the noise? Does it help? Well, as you may have noticed, that depends. It depends on what your fingers are connected to. If you can make your fingers vibrate, you just may hear more than you expected.

WHAT YOU NEED

~ two 18-inch (45-cm) pieces of string

~ metal hanger

WHAT YOU DO

1. Tie one end of both pieces of string to the top of the hanger's hook.

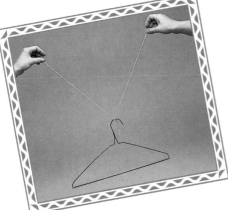

2. Wrap the free ends of both pieces of string around your fingers and place your fingers very gently just barely inside each ear.

3. Walk around the room, allowing the hanger to swing gently against various large, unbreakable objects, such as tables and chairs.

4. Remove your fingers from your ears and allow the hanger to swing against the same objects. Can you still hear the sounds?

WHAT HAPPENED?

When the hanger made contact with the various objects, it began to vibrate and created a sound. The sound moved up the

Sound vibrations travel up the strings, through your fingers, and into your ears.

string to your ears. If the string was stretched slightly, the sound vibrations could travel along the string faster than they would through the air. These vibrations go into your fingers and then into the ear canal. If you were pressing firmly with your fingers, the sound entered your ear through both your eardrums and through the bones in your head. When your fingers are in your ears, you make a more direct connection between the source of the sound and your hearing apparatus, so the sounds are much louder than when your fingers are not in your ears.

SONIC BOOMS

A funny thing happens when a plane goes faster than the speed of sound. In 1889, an Austrian physicist named Ernest Mach created a system of numbers for measuring "supersonic" speeds, or speeds that are faster than the speed of sound. This is why when a plane moves faster than the speed of sound, its speed is referred to as **Mach 1**. But it wasn't until 1947 that someone actually traveled faster than the speed of sound. In his United States Air Force plane, pilot Chuck Yeager became the first person to break the sound barrier. As his plane flew faster than the speed of sound, a huge noise was heard on the ground. This became known as a "sonic boom." As the plane traveled, it pushed the air in front of it, compressing the air into waves. As the plane broke through these waves, it made a very loud, explosive noise. You can experience travel at supersonic speeds if you go on a plane trip on the Concorde, a commercial airplane that travels faster than the speed of sound.

Shake, Rattle, and Roll

Your ears can tell you what direction sounds come from, and in varying situations they also perceive—or take in and understand—sounds differently. As you get older, you tend to lose your ability to hear high-pitched noises. People that live in big cities, or spend time in other environments where there is a lot of very loud noise, such as mines or certain kinds of factories, may experience damage to their ears over time. People who avoid very loud noises tend not to lose their hearing as they age. So, listen up! Let's see what you can hear.

WHAT YOU NEED

 16 to 20 empty cans or containers you can't see through, with lids

~ tablespoon

~ beans, rice, sugar, lentils, sand, buttons, and handfuls of other small materials that can fit inside the containers

~ masking tape

~ pen or pencil

~ paper

~ friends

~ adult helper (optional)

WHAT YOU DO

1. Fill each of two containers with a tablespoon of the same material. Use a small piece of masking tape and a pen or pencil to label the bottom of the jar indicating its contents. Seal the

opening of each jar with the lid. This is one "sound pair."

2. Fill the remaining containers in the same manner, so that you will have eight to ten "sound pairs."

3. Mix up the containers, so that you don't know which pairs match.

4. Take turns with your friends shaking the containers and trying to match up the pairs. Play a

Setup to create one "sound pair."

game by having your friends try to guess the contents of the containers.

5. Try this with an adult helper. If you have a grandparent or other person who is over the age of sixty who can help, you'll be able to discover even more doing this experiment.

Shaking "sound pairs" filled with different materials will test your powers of sound identification.

WHAT HAPPENED?

You were probably surprised to find that you and your friends had no difficulty matching up the pairs. Your ears were sensitive enough to pick up the fine differences in the sounds you created when shaking the containers. The adult helper may have had some difficulty identifying the various contents, and if an even older person gave it a try, he or she probably had even more difficulty. This is because the shaking sounds are quite high-pitched, and as you age you tend to lose the ability to hear higher-pitched sounds.

HOW LOUD IS TOO LOUD?

Sound can be pretty intense. In fact, intensity is the term used to describe the amount of energy contained in sound waves. The more intense a sound is, the louder it will seem to you when you hear it. The intensity of sound is measured in bels (B), units of a measurement named after scientist and inventor Alexander Graham Bell (1847–1922). Most sounds are described in terms of 1/10ths of a bel, or a decibel (dB). For each increase in intensity of 10 decibels, the sound appears to be about twice as loud. Any noise over 120 decibels can be painful and can cause permanent damage to your ears.

Your favorite rock singer may suffer from a hearing loss after years of playing loud music. Rock concerts frequently reach levels of over 120 decibels. Even a sound of 80 decibels can damage your hearing if you listen to it for a long period of time.

If you have to be around loud sounds, you should wear ear protection, either earplugs or earmuffs. Be very careful when you wear a personal stereo set that the volume is set to a safe level, because blasting loud music into your ears for long periods of time will damage your hearing. Also, never put anything except your fingers or earplugs into your ears.

The chart below will give you an idea of how loud some things around you every day are.

Leaves in a light wind	0–10 dB
Quiet conversation	20–50 dB
Loud conversation	50–65 dB
Toilet flushing	67 dB
Vacuum cleaner	70 dB
Hair dryer	80 dB
Heavy traffic	90 dB
Thunder	90–110 dB
Car without a muffler	100 dB
Rock concert	100–120 dB
Airplane taking off	110–200 dB
Space shuttle lift-off	200 dB

Say "Ah!"

When you have a cold, does your voice sound funny? When you try to explain why you sound funny, does the sentence sound like this: " I gotta code id by dose!" There's a reason for that. You normally think of sound coming from your mouth or entering through your ears. What does your nose have to do with all this noise? It turns out your nose and throat have a lot to do with the sound coming from your mouth. This next activity will give you a big surprise.

WHAT YOU NEED

➤ mirror

WHAT YOU DO

1. Stand in front of the mirror and watch your mouth and throat closely as you make the following sounds. Say each of the sounds very slowly, drawing out the sound as if you were singing it.

> Ay (as in "say")
> Ee (as in "see")
> Ii (as in "eye")
> Oo (as in "owe")
> Uu (as in "you")
> Kk (as in "cat")
> Mm (as in "much")

2. Say each of the sounds again, but pinch your nose just after you begin to say the sound. Does this change the sound?

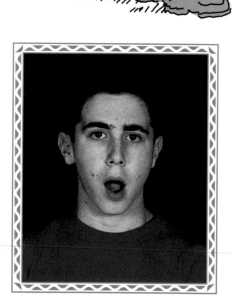

"Oo" and other vowel sounds come more from your larynx and mouth.

The "Mm" sound comes more from your larynx and nose.

40

Pinch your nose and you can't make certain sounds.

WHAT HAPPENED?

You discovered that when you pinched your nose you couldn't say the "Mm" sound and the "Kk" sound changed pitch. Your voice comes from your mouth, your nose, and a part of your throat called your **larynx**. Some sounds, like the "Ay" and "Ee" sounds, come more from your larynx and mouth. Other sounds, like the "Mm" sound, come more from your larynx and nose. The sounds you make vibrate inside your head before coming out. When you made the "Kk" sound and pinched your nose, you increased the pitch because you lost some of that vibration.

SOUND CONTROL

When you take in a breath and make a sound, you are using several different structures inside your body. Your lungs take in the air, which is forced into your throat by the action of your **diaphragm.** The diaphragm is a dome-shaped muscular structure that stretches across your body between your lungs and your abdomen. When it tightens up, it forces the air out of your lungs very quickly, allowing your voice to be quite loud. Once this air is forced into your throat it passes through your larynx. This structure, sometimes called the "voice box," is inside your throat. If you place your hand against the front of your throat and hum, you can feel its vibrations. The larynx contains a pair of elastic **vocal cords** that are controlled by three sets of muscles. When you alter the pitch of your voice from low to high, you use these muscles to shorten and change the shape of your vocal cords. The air moves through a valve at the back of your throat called the **epiglottis**, which closes when you eat or drink so that food can't go down the wrong way. The sound then enters your mouth and nose, where it can be further altered by the position of your tongue and lips. Finally, the sound comes out into the air to be heard by the people around you.

Vocal "Chords"

You may not be used to thinking about your voice as if it were a musical instrument, but you are already able to play a few notes with it. Tuck in your chin, take a deep breath, and make a low-pitched noise. Now lift up your chin, take another breath, and make a high-pitched noise (not too high, remember the neighbors!). How did you do that?

WHAT YOU NEED

⌣ balloon

WHAT YOU DO

1. Inflate the balloon and hold the sides of the neck of the balloon between your thumbs and index fingers.

2. Stretch the neck of the balloon gently and allow some of the air to escape.

3. Pull back and forth on the neck of the balloon to alter the amount of air that is leaving and the size of

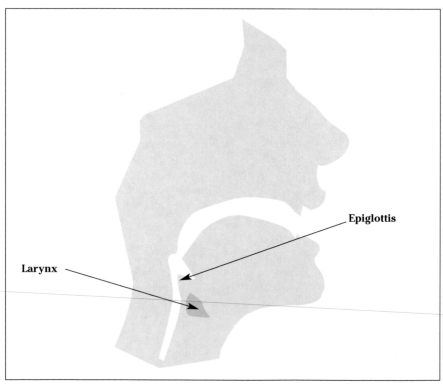

Epiglottis

Larynx

the opening. Listen to the different sounds this makes.

WHAT HAPPENED?

When the air escaped from the neck of the balloon, it made a shrieking sound. As you stretched and released the opening, the sound changed to a lower or higher pitch. The neck of the balloon acted like your vocal cords. Your vocal cords contract or tighten to make higher-pitched sounds, and expand or loosen to make lower-pitched sounds. Your fingers acted like the muscles of your larynx, tightening and loosening the vocal cords to alter the pitch of the sound. Different balloons will make slightly different sounds. This is also true of different larynxes. In general, men have deeper voices than women because they have longer and thicker vocal cords. Men's voices have a peak frequency of about 125 Hz, while that of an average woman's voice is about 250 Hz. Children's voices are at even higher frequencies. Boys and girls have voices in the same range until puberty, when the vocal cords of boys grow much more than those of girls. Vocal *cords* are part of your body; vocal *chords* refers to singing a chord, which is made up three or more different musical notes sounded at the same time.

SONGS FROM THE DEEP

Whales sing. Not rock music, but songs only they understand. The sounds that whales make vary depending on which other whale a whale is communicating with, and what information the whale is sending. Whales can sing specific "mating songs" which last up to twenty minutes and can be repeated throughout the day. Pods (groups) of whales have their own songs, which change throughout the season and over the years. Certain kinds of whales, such as humpback and fin whales, can send their songs over long distances. Fin whales send out a loud, low sound that can be heard even thousands of miles away. Scientists believe that the depth at which the whale sends a sound, combined with the water pressure, temperature, and the amount of salt in the water through which the sound is being sent, is what enables a whale's message to be heard over vast distances.

Off the coast of western Canada, there is a unique radio station that plays only whale "music"! Researchers have stationed microphones at different locations frequented by whales. The sensitive microphones pick up the whale songs, which are then transmitted by radio waves. The best part is that the station doesn't need to pause for commercial breaks or even pay a deejay!

Whales sing "songs" that only other whales can understand.
Photo by John Ford. Courtesy of Vancouver Aquarium.

Mystery Voices

A funny thing happens when you make a cassette recording of you and your friends. When you hear the recording of your friend's voice, it sounds perfectly normal. When you hear your own voice, it sounds very odd, like someone else. When you hear yourself on the cassette, you might say to yourself: "Who said that? Someone must have snuck in and changed the cassette!" But it really is your voice. You are just hearing it in a different way.

WHAT YOU DO

1. Read aloud the introduction to this project while recording your voice. Then record your friends' voices while they read aloud the same introduction.

WHAT YOU NEED

➤ cassette recorder and blank cassette

➤ several friends

➤ paper

➤ pencils

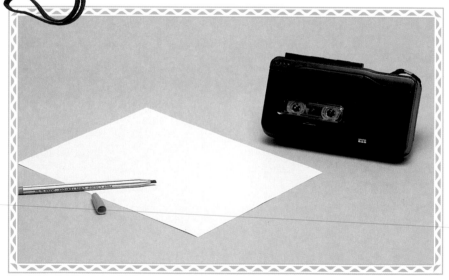

Identifying recorded voices may be trickier than you think!

2. Rewind the cassette and play short sections of each person's recorded speech. Change the order in which you play them from the order in which you recorded them. Have each of your friends identify the different speakers by writing their names on a piece of paper.

3. Compare their guesses with the actual speakers in each case.

WHAT HAPPENED?

Though it seems very strange, people are often better at identifying other peoples' voices than they are at recognizing their own! Hearing the recorded speech is more like hearing someone else's voice, because you hear the recorded sound

ELEPHANT LOVE CALLS

Even if you recognized your own voice in the experiment you just did, you might not be able to recognize an elephant love call. Elephants use infrasound to communicate over large distances with other members of their herd. This initially puzzled scientists because they saw the elephants respond to the messages, but the researchers couldn't hear the sounds. Elephants make low, rumbling sounds in their throats, and the sound is made louder in the large hollow cavities of the elephant's head. The sound blasts outwards and can be heard miles away by other elephants.

only through your ears. You hear your real voice through your ears, but also through the bones in your skull that conduct

sound vibrations to your inner ear. You have tiny muscles in your middle ear that dampen or decrease your hearing when you begin to speak. This helps you from being bothered by the loud sound of your own voice.

MUSIC TO MY EARS

What is the difference between "music" and "noise"? And when does music become noise? Noise is a random sound that has irregular sound waves. The sound of a cymbal or drumbeat is about as close as a musical instrument gets to making "noise." If you could take a picture of a musical note, you would see that it has regular waves that repeat themselves. To give you an idea of what noise is, try this: Set your television on a channel playing music you like. You can hear pleasing sounds, right? Now turn the television past the last channel on which you can receive a signal. You should have a blank picture with static and fuzzy sound: noise. Flip back to the music channel and the sounds are nice to listen to once again. Music is sound that is in a pattern that people can hear or discern. Music can be sung, or played on an instrument, or even produced by nature.

In this section, you will learn something about the history of music, why some sounds are more pleasing to listen to than others, and why certain violins sound better than others. You'll even learn how singers break a glass using only their voices!

That Doggone Talent!

Have you ever heard music so beautiful it made the hair on the back of your neck stand up? Really fine opera singers have the ability to do some special things with their voices. They can inspire and entertain you. They can even break drinking glasses with the sound of their voices. They sing at higher and lower pitches than most people can manage. Something really weird happens if they use their voices to produce very high-pitched sounds. Let's see what it is.

WHAT YOU NEED

- ➻ piano (optional)
- ➻ recording of opera (optional)

WHAT YOU DO

1. Play the lowest note on the piano. See if you can sing the word "dog" at the same pitch as that note. If you don't have a piano, just try to sing "dog" at the lowest pitch your voice can produce.

2. Work your way up the piano playing the white keys, singing the word "dog" at the same pitch that the various keys make when you play them. What happens to the word as you reach the highest notes on the instrument? If

Start by playing the piano's lowest note and singing the word "dog."

As you play higher notes and sing at a higher pitch, something happens to the word "dog."

47

you don't have a piano, just try to sing "dog" at increasingly higher pitches until you make the highest-pitched sound you can. **3.** If you have one, listen to a recording of a woman singing opera. Can you recognize any of the words she is singing when she is singing the high notes?

WHAT HAPPENED?

When you sang the word "dog" in a pitch that matched the lower, or deeper-pitched, notes made by piano keys, you could clearly understand which word you were singing. As you began to sing the word at higher and higher pitches, you couldn't actually make out the word "dog" anymore. It just sounded like the note. This is because different sounds in our speech have certain characteristic frequencies. For example, the "ee" sound in the word "speed" is higher in pitch than the "ou" sound in the word "ouch." When you sang the word at higher pitches, you eventually reached a pitch where the sounds ran together and you couldn't hear the word properly anymore.

In "Hey Pitcher, Pitcher!" (see page 17), you learned that low-pitched sounds come from low-frequency vibrations and high-pitched sounds from high-frequency vibrations. But your mind tells you if one pitch or

Photo by David Cooper. Courtesy of Vancouver Opera.

sound is better or more pleasing than another of similar pitch. Without music to sing along with, most people won't hit exactly the right notes. But there are some people with perfect pitch, which means they can sing a given note even without the background music. Many really good opera singers have perfect pitch. Singers are sometimes grouped together by the range of notes they can sing.

Here are some of the names used to describe people who sing in different ranges, and the ranges of frequencies in which they sing:

Soprano—262 to 1047 Hz
Alto—196 to 698 Hz
Tenor—147 to 523 Hz
Baritone—110 to 392 Hz
Bass—82 to 294 Hz

Trained singers can also change the frequency of a note or the loudness of a note. When they change the frequency slightly in a rhythmic way, it is referred to as *vibrato*. When they change the note's volume, or loudness, it is called *tremolo*. As singers age, their voices change, and their high-end range decreases.

You can hear opera singers' voices above the sound of the orchestra accompanying them because their timbre or quality is unique.

Stretched to the Limit

Pythagoras was a Greek scientist who lived in the sixth century B.C. In addition to coming up with a famous theorem about triangles, he was renowned for his work on the subject of musical scales. Pythagoras described the link between mathematics and music. He used something called a **monochord**, a primitive musical instrument with a single string under tension with a moveable bridge. You can make your own monochord and see if you can discover what Pythagoras observed.

WHAT YOU NEED

- ➤ adult helper
- ➤ piece of wood 1 to 2 inches (2.5 to 5.0 cm) thick × 3 feet (90 cm) long × 4 inches (10 cm) wide
- ➤ 3-inch (7.5-cm) nail
- ➤ hammer
- ➤ 2 tubes of lipstick of the same diameter
- ➤ duct tape or electrical tape
- ➤ 4-foot-long (120-cm) fishing line
- ➤ pail with handle
- ➤ marbles, small rocks, or sand

WHAT YOU DO

1. Have your adult helper hammer the nail into the piece of wood about one inch (2.5 cm) from one end of the piece of wood. He or she should try to center the nail in the middle of the wood, then place the nailed

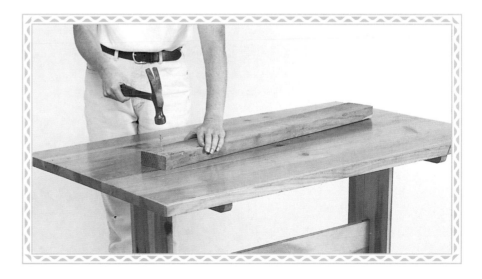

piece of wood on a flat surface such as a table.

2. Have your helper tie one end of the fishing line firmly to the nail. Run the fishing line down to the opposite end of the wooden block so that it dangles over the edge of the table.

3. Tie the other end of the fishing line to the handle of the pail. The pail should be able to swing freely. Pluck the fishing line. Do you hear any sound?

4. Place one lipstick tube under the fishing line close to the nail, and a second lipstick tube under the fishing line about 3 inches (7.5 cm) from the other end of the wooden block. These will serve as your bridges. You may wish to use a small strip of tape to hold the lipstick in place. Now try plucking the fishing line in its center. What sound does it make now?

5. Add some marbles, small rocks, or sand to the pail, and pluck the string. Did the sound change with each added weight?

6. Move the lipstick tubes to various places on the wooden block. Did this make any difference to the sound produced when the string is plucked?

WHAT HAPPENED?

When you plucked the string, you created a **standing wave**. In a standing wave, there are still areas called **nodes** and areas with a lot of movement called **antinodes**. The nodes in the system you created are the points where the string touches the lipstick tubes. There is an antinode in the center of the string. The vibration of the string caused the sound you heard. If you kept the weight the same and moved the lipstick tubes, the sound changed as the tubes got close together. The sound produced was at a higher pitch as the distance in the fishing line got shorter. This is because a shorter section of the fishing line was vibrating. When you added rocks to the pail, but kept the distance between the lipstick tubes the same, the sound produced was also at a higher pitch. This is because the section of fishing line had more tension on it. It was tighter and vibrated at a higher frequency.

Pythagoras found that he could use the various bridge positions to compare the intervals formed when two string segments were plucked. He discovered that with segments of equal lengths, he heard the same note. Pythagoras also found that when the ratio of the length of the segments was 2 to 1, the interval between the notes is what we now call an

octave. He also examined the ratio of 4 to 3, which is called the **fourth**, and the ratio of 3 to 2, which is called a **fifth**.

When notes an octave apart are played, they sound so much like each other that you probably won't be able to tell there are two notes being played. Notes an octave apart on the piano are twelve notes apart when both black and white keys are counted. We say that there are twelve **semitones (S)** in an octave. The sequence of notes starting with one note on the piano and playing all the keys until you come to the same note again, an interval of thirteen notes, is called a **chromatic scale**. Two semitones occurring at the same interval equal one tone (T). A diatonic major scale is a sequence of eight notes, starting anywhere on the keyboard and in the pattern TTSTTTS where the T's are the tones and the S's are the semitones. The easiest scale to play is the C major scale, where you play only the white keys from C to C. When you change the note, you begin playing on, you change to a different "key." A fifth is the interval between the key note or first note of a scale and the fifth note on the scale, a total of five notes. Ancient Chinese music was based on the fifth rather than the octave. Fifths were also common in other early music. Gregorian chants, for example, have harmonies sung only at fifths and octaves.

You Can Tune a Piano, but You Can't Tuna Fish

This next activity is "fundamental" to all music. The **fundamental** is the lowest frequency of each note that an instrument can produce. As you saw in "Stretched to the Limit" (see page 49), when a string vibrates, it produces higher and lower notes. This next activity will give you an idea of where scales came from and the theory behind them.

WHAT YOU NEED

~ 25 feet (7.6 meters) of rope

~ door with a doorknob

WHAT YOU DO

1. Tie the end of the rope to the doorknob.

2. Hold the free end of the rope in your hand and stand far enough from the door so that the rope is taut.

3. Slowly move your hand up and down, so the rope begins to form a wave from your hand to the door and back again.

4. Gradually get the wave to move faster by changing the speed of the up-and-down movements of your hand.

5. The rope may begin to show several visible waves at the same time in different sections. See how many of these waves you can produce at any one time.

WHAT HAPPENED?

When the rope first began to move, it moved up and down in

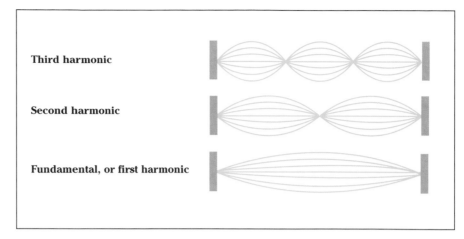

one motion as a single curve, like half of a wave. As you began to move the rope faster, you saw distinct sections of waves. You created standing waves between your hand and the doorknob. What does that have to do with sound, you might ask? Standing waves are really important when it comes to music. When a string in a stringed instrument such as a guitar is plucked or bowed or struck, it also creates standing waves. It does this at several frequencies simultaneously. The first frequency is called the fun-

damental or first harmonic, and it is the lowest-pitched sound. The second frequency is twice as fast as the first frequency and is called the second harmonic. Each additional harmonic frequency that you may hear is an integer multiple of the fundamental. These harmonics sound good together. The harmonic frequencies correspond to the length ratios seen by Pythagorus (see "Stretched to the Limit," page 49). Similarly, in wind instruments the sound waves inside the instrument form standing waves and create

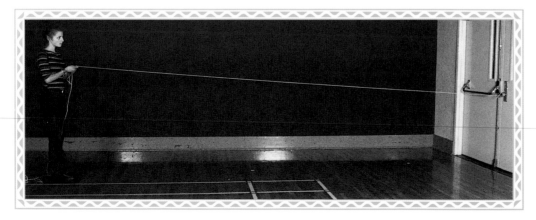

Changing the speed of your hand's motions will create different types of wave.

harmonics. Depending on the type of instrument you play, you may be hearing only some of the harmonics.

If the rope were a string of a musical instrument, that first half-wave would be the string vibrating at its fundamental frequency, or first harmonic. When the string is vibrating in two sections, this would translate into a note that is twice the frequency, which is the second harmonic. The second harmonic is a tone an octave higher than the fundamental or the lowest note. The third harmonic is three times the fundamental frequency or a note with a pitch an octave and a fifth above the fundamental.

Spouting Bowl

If you've never heard of a rather odd and wonderful thing called the "spouting bowl," you're about to learn something fun. The "spouting bowl" was invented in China in the fifth century, and it offers a great demonstration of a standing wave. When it is filled with water and its metal handles are rubbed, it produces a low, humming sound. The vibrations from this hum cause the water to bubble up in a fine mist. The water spouts only when the noise from the bowl is at a particular frequency. The broader the chest of the person rubbing the handles, the higher the bubbles will rise above the surface of the water. You may not be able purchase these bowls where you live, but you can do a similar experiment to illustrate standing waves.

WHAT YOU NEED

~ crystal wine glass

~ water

WHAT YOU DO

1. Ask your parents for permission to use a fine crystal wine glass. You will need a glass with very thin sides. Fill the glass with water until there is a space of about ½ inch (1 cm) from the top.
2. Place the glass on a table. Dip your index finger into the water.
3. Hold the stem of your glass firmly between the fingers of your dry hand. Run your wetted finger around the rim of the glass. You should hear a humming sound.
4. Vary the speed at which you run your finger around the rim. How does that affect the wave in the water and the sound you make?

Spouting bowl from Beijing, China.

Rubbing the metal handles creates a standing wave inside the bowl.

Rubbing the rim of a crystal wine glass produces a result similar to that of the spouting bowl.

5. Change the level of the water in the glass by taking a few sips. Run your finger around the glass again. Did it make the same sound?

WHAT HAPPENED?

When you ran your finger around the rim of the glass, you heard a sound. That sound had a certain characteristic pitch, depending on the glass and the amount of water it contained. You may have heard a slightly higher-pitched sound when you drank some of the water. If you were lucky, at some point the water even bubbled up like the water in the spouting bowl. You created a standing wave in the glass. A standing wave is created when two identical waves move past each other in opposite directions. The two waves mix together so that there are still areas called nodes and areas with a lot of movement called antinodes.

MUSICAL SCALES AND MUSIC NOTATION

Musical scales didn't just come into being all at once: they actually evolved over many years. There is some evidence that people have been playing musical notes for over 35,000 years. Scales probably began as a way for musicians to begin playing together. Many scales that still exist are made of notes at quite different intervals from those we now use. Some of these scales came from the design of the instruments used to play them. For example, if a flute is made with evenly spaced holes, the scales you can play on it sound quite strange to our ears.

More than 5,000 years ago the Chinese established a scale based on intervals of a fifth, called the five-tone pentatonic scale. Musicians tuned early multi-stringed and keyboard instruments so that they "sounded right." Unfortunately, when the musicians wanted to change the key they were playing in (see "Stretched to the Limit," page 49), they needed to retune the instruments. The modern scale was developed, at least in part, to allow people to play keyboard instruments in different keys.

Let's start with the basics: A chromatic scale involves playing in order all the notes (for example, both white and black keys on a piano), through one octave. "Octave" refers to the eight natural notes you play. As you can see by looking at a piano keyboard, there are twelve keys or notes that fall within one octave, eight white keys that play the natural notes, and five black keys that play notes called sharps and flats. In the modern, equal-tempered scale, the frequency of any note on the keyboard divided by the frequency of the note that follows below is about 1.06.

Is It Live?

Did you know that you can use sound to break a crystal glass? The glass will begin to vibrate when exposed to sound at its fundamental frequency. This vibration is called **resonance.** If the singer sings at this frequency with enough volume for a few seconds, the vibrations will become powerful enough to cause the glass to break. Unfortunately, you can do this only if you have a very powerful voice and if you use an extremely expensive, thin-walled glass, so don't try it at home! This experiment won't teach you how to break a glass with your singing, but it will teach you about resonance.

WHAT YOU NEED

- piano
- whistle
- guitar
- two identical wide-mouthed pop bottles
- adult helper

WHAT YOU DO

1. Have an adult open the top of the piano so the strings are exposed. Press down on the "sustain" pedal.

2. Play a whistle near the keys. Do any piano strings start to vibrate?

3. Try this again, this time by playing different strings on the

guitar. What notes vibrate on the piano this time?

4. Try yelling onto the piano strings. Now what happens?

5. Hold the mouth of a bottle next to one of your ears. Have a friend stand several feet away from you and blow across the top of another bottle to make a whistling sound. What did you hear in your bottle?

WHAT HAPPENED?

It seemed as though the piano was having a duet with the other instruments. The piano strings began to vibrate when certain notes were played. The guitar caused certain strings on the piano to vibrate, while the whistle and your voice caused other strings to vibrate. Each of the instruments vibrated at specific frequencies. Likewise, when your friend blew across the top of the bottle, you heard a noise inside your bottle. Since the bottles are identical, they vibrate with the same fundamental frequency. This phenomenon is known as "sympathetic vibration."

When playing musical instruments, resonance causes a sound to be played louder, or longer, or to be changed in tone. In the instruments, the sounds you made caused the strings to vibrate along with the sound. The strings that vibrate are the strings that produce sounds with the same frequencies as the whistle and your voice. The wine glass we mentioned earlier breaks because the sound causes a standing wave to form at the resonant frequency of the glass. The wine glass is brittle, and changing its shape causes it to shatter.

MUSIC NOTATION

We describe some people who play instruments as playing them "by ear." This generally means they can hear a song and play it back without reading any music. Most classical musicians read music. Musicians in orchestras, for example, must read music in order to coordinate their playing with that of their fellow performers. The method used for writing music down is called **notation.** The notes above or higher than middle C are written on five lines called the treble clef. You can tell it's the treble clef because it will have this symbol at the beginning of the music: 𝄞. The notes below or lower than middle C are on the bass clef, which has this symbol at the beginning of the music: 𝄢.

Western music (not country-and-western music, but the kind of music that originated in Europe) is measured. It has a certain number of **beats** in a given amount of time, better known as a bar or measure. When you see music written, there are often notes that are completely black. Other notes are joined together by lines on the top or bottom of the note, while still others are empty circles. These notes look strange for a reason. The way that a note is written tells you not only which pitch the note should be played in, but also how long the note should last. Musicians must do math each time they play in order to figure out how many notes to play in each section of time.

Eastern or Oriental music works a little differently. It is based on speech patterns and is meant to mimic the way people speak. It's often taught by using words that represent the notes or beat, instead of written music.

Western music is based on measured time, which is nothing like the way that people speak. An example of speaking in measured time would be the way a Shakespearean sonnet sounds. Ask your parents or teachers to read a sonnet aloud and you'll immediately hear the difference between language written or spoken in standard, everyday speech and language written or spoken in measured time.

Timber!

If you play a musical instrument in a band, you know that different instruments sound different from each other. You can tell a violin from a saxophone by listening to them being played. The sound quality that allows you to tell these instruments apart is called **timbre,** which looks like it should be pronounced "timber" but is actually pronounced "tamber." (And while we're on this subject: "bass" is pronounced "base," not "bass" like the fish.) Musical instruments sound different from each other because of their timbre. Try this experiment and see what differences you hear.

WHAT YOU NEED

❧ various musical instruments such as: piano, guitar, violin, cello, clarinet, recorder, saxophone (or a synthesizer or electronic keyboard)

❧ helpers

WHAT YOU DO

1. Have each musician start by playing the middle C note. Do the instruments produce the same sound?
2. Have each musician play the C scale. Do they sound the same?
3. Have each musician play the C scale at the same time. Which instrument do you hear the most? Which makes the softest sound?

WHAT HAPPENED?

When you played the same note on different instruments, at the same pitch and level or intensity, the notes did not sound the same. This is because although each instrument plays the same note, the sounds have different timbres. Each instrument plays the fundamental frequency and the different harmonics (see "Spouting Bowl," page 53). What gives the notes different timbres is that the loudness of each of the harmonics varies, as does the number of harmonics you can hear. If you were to play the same note on a violin, a flute, a saxophone, a piano, and a cello, you would hear different amounts of harmonic frequencies in the sound each one makes. For example, if you plucked the same note on a banjo with a pick and used your fingers on a harp, you would find that the banjo sounds "twangy" while the harp sounds soft. The banjo has more of the higher frequencies, which gives it that metallic tone. The musical

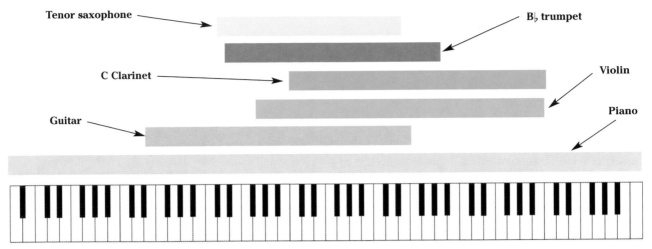

Musicians use a variety of instruments to play notes in different ranges. Some, like the piano, have a wide range, while others, like a bell, will only play a single note.

sound of a flute sounds soft and pure because you hear very few of the harmonics. Many things come together to create timbre. The materials used, and the quality of the materials combined with such things as even the shape of the player's lips on woodwind's mouthpiece, can all affect the sound. Another thing that affects timbre is the way the sound is created in the instru-

ment. The sound a drum makes will be different depending on what part of the drumhead is struck. Likewise, a violin sounds different depending on where on its string the bow is applied.

The ancient Chinese were the first to understand timbre. In the third century A.D., they created an instrument called the *ku ch'in*, or zither, which had five, seven, or sometimes even nine

strings. The nodes of vibration were marked on the board and the strings were played in such a way that the pitch did not change, but different harmonics for each string were produced. The strings were made from silk, and the zither took years of practice to learn to play. A player needed to learn twenty-six different ways to pluck or stroke for one kind of note!

WHY A STRADIVARIUS VIOLIN IS SO EXPENSIVE

No one knows how Antonio Stradivari, the famous maker of violins (1644–1737), made his instruments, and no one was able to recreate the quality of his work for hundreds of years. Some people claim it was because of the wood he used, while others believe it was the resin or lacquer coating the instrument. Still others think the exceptional quality of his violins relied on the way they were carved or constructed. One thing is for certain: For over 260 years, these violins have kept their reputation for amazingly good timbre and resonance. There are only about a thousand of these violins still known to exist, and they are sought after and treasured by both violinists and collectors.

Pick-Up Sticks

Some sounds are really pleasant, while other sounds make you want to plug your ears. If notes sound pleasant when played together, we say they are "consonant" or harmonious. If notes clash or sound inharmonious, we say they have **dissonance** or are "dissonant." In "Stretched to the Limit" (see page 49), you learned that notes that are a fifth apart (such as C and G) are consonant. In this activity, you won't need an instrument to make some dissonant noise.

WHAT YOU NEED

ᕀ 8 pieces of ½-inch (1.25-cm) wooden doweling of different lengths (at 1-inch [2.5-cm] intervals from 5 inches [12.5 cm] to 14 inches [35.5 cm])

ᕀ 10 pieces of ½-inch (1.25-cm) wooden doweling of the same length (about 9 inches [22.5 cm]

ᕀ wood, tiled, or stone floor

ᕀ piano (optional)

WHAT YOU DO

1. Drop the ten same-sized pieces of wooden doweling onto the floor at the same time. What kind of noise does this produce?

2. Now drop the ten different-sized pieces of doweling on the floor at the same time. What kind of noise does this make?

3. If you have a piano, play the

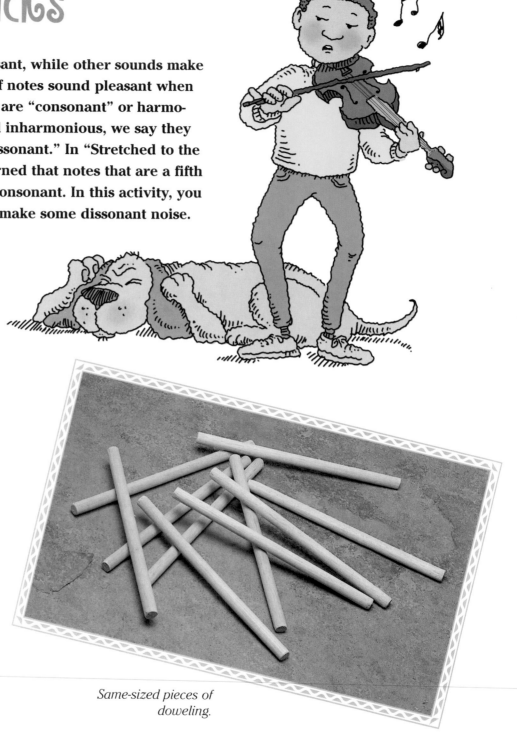

Same-sized pieces of doweling.

Different-sized pieces of doweling.

C and E notes at the same time, or the C and G notes. Now try playing C and D♭ or C and G♭. Which pairs of notes sound pleasant? Which pairs sound terrible?

WHAT HAPPENED?

When you dropped the different-sized sticks at the same time, each stick produced a different tone when it hit the floor. The differences in these tones made the sticks sound more musical. When you dropped the same-sized sticks, it made a terrible sound.

WHITE NOISE AND ANTINOISE

You know that there is something called "noise." But do you know that there is also something called **antinoise?**" Sound, as you know, has waves. These waves can be described as " in phase" or "out of phase" (reversed) with each other. If you add together two out-of-phase waves at the right frequency, the result is silence. One way to prove this is by using a special computer; a microphone picks up the sound and sends it back to the computer. This computer reads the waves and makes a "mirror image," or reverse copy, of the wave. The wave is then played back against the original sound. When the two waves meet, they overlap each other exactly at the high and low peaks; this eliminates the sound, creating zero sound. **White noise**, on the other hand, is made up of sound waves of all frequencies. It can sound very peaceful, like a waterfall, and people find it very relaxing to listen to. People who don't like rooms that are quiet often purchase white noise machines that create these relaxing sounds to listen to.

INSTRUMENTAL ACCOMPANIMENT

Now that you know something about sound, you're ready to learn about the physics of music. There's a ton of science involved in how music is made, and how musical instruments work!

One way to start thinking about the science of music and instruments is to simply take a look at your classmates. Even though you all look different from each other, you still have similar characteristics—you wouldn't ever mistake one of your friends for a cat, or a dolphin, or a spider! This is because you are all from the same biological "family," the family of human beings.

It works much the same way with musical instruments. Each instrument is from a certain family, and instruments that are in the same family share like characteristics—parts that work in a similar way to make the instrument produce music. The main families of instruments and some of the instruments they include are: string (guitar, cello); woodwind (flute, clarinet); brass (trumpet, french horn); and percussion (drums, piano).

In this section, you will learn about what happens inside a musical instrument that allows it to produce music.

Band on the Run

Imagine your favorite rock or pop singer standing up on stage playing an old-fashioned instrument instead of an electric guitar. It would look pretty silly, wouldn't it? But the guitar—and its cousin the banjo—evolved from the *lute*, a fifteenth-century European instrument with five pairs of strings. (The lute itself evolved from its ancestor the *ud*, an ancient north African instrument with four pairs of strings.) The kind of guitar with which we are most familiar was designed by a Spanish guitar maker named Antonio de Torres Jurado (1817–1892). This guitar had a flat back, metal frets (bars embedded in the wooden neck of the guitar), and 26-inch (65-cm) strings, and was about the same size as the instrument used by most musicians today. Here's an activity to teach you why a guitar works the way it does.

WHAT YOU NEED

∾ 4 rubber bands of the same diameter but different widths

∾ guitar

∾ small tissue box

∾ chopsticks or pencils

WHAT YOU DO

1. Stretch a rubber band between your thumb and your index finger. Pluck the rubber band with your other hand while changing the distance between your thumb and finger. What happens to the pitch of the sounds you're making?

2. Choose any string on a guitar and loosen and tighten the

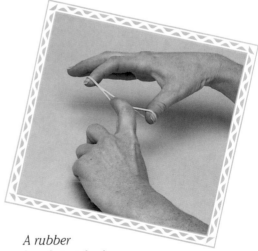

A rubber band stretched between your thumb and index finger produces a sound when plucked.

string by slowly turning the metal peg at the end of the neck of the guitar. Pluck the string while you are changing the tension of the string. Now what happens to the pitch?

3. Stretch four rubber bands around an empty tissue box. Arrange the bands from the thickest to the thinnest. Make

sure the bands are placed over the hole in the box.
4. Slide the chopstick or pencil under the rubber bands, and position one at either end of the box, close to the edge. This is the instrument's bridge.
5. Pluck or strum the rubber bands. How does the different thickness of the different rubber bands affect the sound?

WHAT HAPPENED?

When you stretched the rubber band between your fingers and plucked it, you produced a sound. When you pulled the rubber band tighter, the sound may have been slightly higher pitched. You probably noticed that the band became longer as you pulled it. A longer band gives a lower pitch, so the tightness and length work in opposition to each other. When you kept the length and tension of the bands the same and stretched them around the box you learned something else about bands and pitch. The thicker the string plucked, the lower the pitch. Thicker strings have more mass so they vibrate more slowly, and the lower frequency of sound they produce

Properly assembled tissue-box "guitar."

has a lower pitch. The strings of guitars are all about the same length, and they are tuned so that they are near the same tension for easy playing. What makes the guitar strings produce different notes is the different mass of the strings: thinner strings produce higher notes than thicker ones. To make heavier strings and produce lower notes, the strings are sometimes wrapped in wire. Three different factors affect the pitch of a stringed instrument: the strings' length, tension, and thickness. If you change one of these things keeping the other two the same, the pitch decreases when either the length or thickness increases; pitch increases with increased tension.

"STRINGED" INSTRUMENTS

You've probably noticed that the word "string" doesn't precisely describe the long, skinny parts you pluck or strum on a guitar. "Stringed instruments" aren't actually fitted with string. Early stringed instruments were fitted with pieces of gut. Nowadays, their "strings" are made from nylon thread or steel wire of different thicknesses. Typically, classical guitars are fitted with nylon strings and the guitars used to play popular music have steel strings that give a brighter sound. When you tune a guitar, you have to set the fundamental frequency (see "You Can Tune a Piano, but You Can't Tuna Fish," page 51) of each string. As you turn the metal peg attached to the end of each string, you are really changing the tension of the string. As the tension is increased, the string's frequency increases and it will play a higher tone. If you decrease the tension, the frequency also decreases and the string plays a lower tone. Nylon and steel strings are perfect for this use because they are strong enough to be stretched to high tensions.

Knock on Wood

We sometimes "knock on wood" for good luck. People who make violins often knock on wood for a different reason. Traditionally, the front and back plates of violins are carved from solid pieces of wood. As the wood approaches the correct dimensions, the violin maker taps lightly on the wood and listens to the sound it makes. The "tap tones" made by knocking on the wood have a specific pitch. Experienced carvers can use this pitch to tell how thin the wood needs to be in order to make the correct sound when the violin is played. This experiment will teach you a little bit more about why this is true.

WHAT YOU NEED

∾ piece of wood, 1 inch (2.5 cm) thick × 4 inches (10 cm) wide × 2 feet (60 cm) long

∾ 2 chairs

∾ 2 pieces of string, each 5 feet (1.5 m) long

∾ sand

∾ tablespoon

∾ chopstick

∾ cork

WHAT YOU DO

1. Tie one end of each of the strings to the arms or the backs of the chair. Place the second chair about 18 inches (45 cm) from and facing the first chair, and tie the other end of each of the strings to the chair. The strings should hang parallel to each other.

2. Balance the wooden plank across the middle of the strings.

3. Twist the chopstick into the end of the cork to create a baton.

4. Sprinkle about a tablespoon (15 mL) of sand over the wooden plank.

5. Hammer the middle of the top of the wooden plank in a regular beat, using the baton. Watch what happens to the sand.

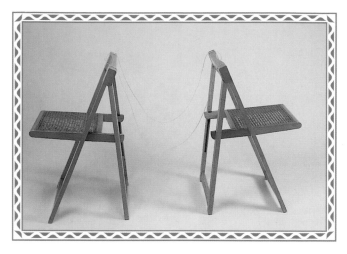

Setup for the experiment.

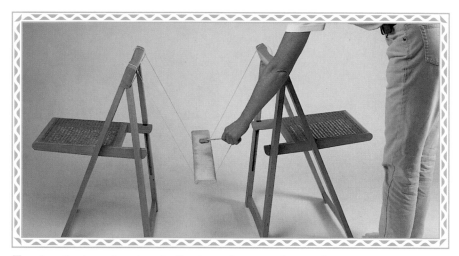

Tapping the board makes it vibrate and moves the sand.

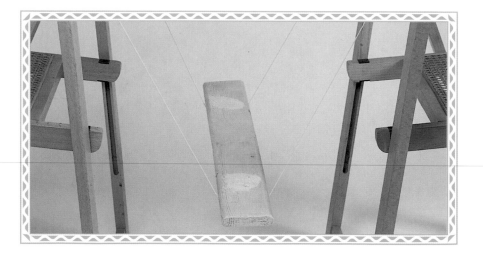

WHAT HAPPENED?

When you tapped the board, it vibrated. The sand moved across the board. Eventually the sand moved into the area above the supporting strings. When the board vibrated, the areas over the strings didn't move as much as the other parts of the board. The areas over the strings are the nodes. Since the sand didn't get vibrated as much in these areas, it settled in the nodes. How does this information apply to musical instruments? They also include wooden pieces that vibrate, and the vibration of these pieces is crucial to how the instrument works. To demonstrate this, Torres (see page 63) made a guitar out of papier mâché. The only wooden part of the case was the soundboard, which is the piece of wood that makes up the front face of the guitar. People were astonished at the quality of the sound produced when this guitar was played. When a guitar is played, both its soundboard and sound box resonate; this makes the notes louder. The wood faces of guitars and violins vibrate and amplify the sound from the strings. Slight differences in the type of wood the instrument is made of and the shape of its soundboard and sound box give each instrument its own unique sound. This is one reason why it is so difficult to duplicate the sound made by a Stradivarius violin (see "Why Is a Stradivarius So Expensive?" page 59).

If you look at a violin you see two holes: one looks like a fancy letter "f" and the other looks like a reversed fancy "f". These are called "sound holes" or "f holes." These designs are there for a reason and not just to make the violin look pretty. When a violinist plays a note, the noise or vibrations travel down the bridge and into the sound box. The sound waves are spread throughout the sound box, which in turn creates a standing wave inside the box. This standing wave amplifies or resonates the sound, which is why the note will sound louder. The waves then use the holes to escape from the sound box. Check out a book on musical instruments and see how many stringed instruments have sound boxes.

Sticky Stuff

What do a playground slide and a violin have in common? You'd be surprised! Have you ever gone down a metal playground slide while wearing shorts or a skirt? If you have, you know that it can hurt a little. The metal slide seems to grab on to your skin and pinch the backs of your thighs. But it doesn't hurt at all when you slide down the slide wearing jeans or pants. Why is this true? This activity will help you find out. It doesn't require you to travel to the playground, nor will you need a musical instrument. You'll just need to make a little trip to the hardware store.

WHAT YOU NEED

~ 3-foot-long (92 cm) piece of aluminum rod, ¼ inch (0.6 cm) in diameter

~ steel wool

~ rosin (from a music store or music teacher)

~ scrap of leather or heavy material

WHAT YOU DO

1. Use the steel wool to thoroughly wipe away any traces of grease and oil that may be on the aluminum rod. Make sure the rod is entirely clean.

2. Experiment with balancing the rod on one of your index fingers until you find a position in which you can balance the rod on your finger. The position

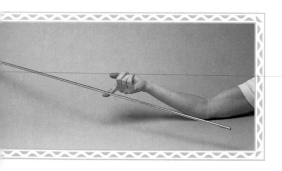

your finger is now in is at the balance point of the rod.

3. Wrap the thumb and fingers of one hand around the rod at the balance point.

4. Coat the leather or material in powdered rosin and wrap this material around the rod next to the balance point.

5. Keeping the coated material wrapped around the rod, run the material in long strokes along the rod from the balance point to the end to create a sound. This will take some practice.

6. Change the starting point of your hand from the balance point to different points on the rod, running the material along the rod from this new point. How does the sound change?

WHAT HAPPENED?

You created a sound when you ran the material along the length of the rod. The rosin on the leather or cloth allowed the cloth to stick slightly to the rod as it was pulled along. This

caused the rod to vibrate. As you held the rod in different positions, you could also raise or lower the sound you created. When longer sections of the rod vibrated, it gave a deeper sound. When you held the rod so that only a short section could vibrate, the sound was higher in pitch. Musical instruments need some sort of sound box to make strings produce louder sounds, but that's not all that goes into making music. In the case of stringed instruments, you also need something to make the strings vibrate. Your fingers do the work with guitars by picking or plucking the strings. When you play a piano key, a hammer hits the string contained in the instrument. With violins, violas, cellos, and the double bass, long bows are used to set the string in motion. The rough horsehair surface of the bow is coated with a sticky material called rosin, which is made from turpentine or the sap of pine trees. The rough hair coated with the sticky material grabs the strings as the bow slides across, causing the strings to vibrate.

The Ringing of Bells

It's hard to find a person who doesn't like the sweet, rich sounds of bells. But how much do you know about bells? Here's a little "bell history" for you. Tuned bells originated in ancient China in around the sixth century B.C. The Chinese used bells for more than their musical qualities (or for calling people home for dinner!). In fact, they based their entire system of measurement on the pitches of bells to determine length, width, weight, and volume. The pitches of bells were changed into units of measure using a 7-foot-long (2.1m) stringed tuner. The tuning of the string was matched to the pitch of the bell. The string was then measured, and its length was used as a standard of measurement. Since these standards had to be identical in different parts of the country to avoid confusion with measurements, bell-making became an important art.

The largest set of ancient chime bells included sixty-four bells and was found in 1978 in Hupei, China. These bells, dating from the fifth century B.C., were finely tuned instruments made of bronze. The bells were mounted on wooden beams, and the largest bell weighed over 100 pounds (45 kg). Inscribed on each bell was a long description of the note it played, where it fit into the scale, and how the government used that scale for measurement.

69

WHAT YOU NEED

~ 8 pieces of ½-inch (1.3-cm) -diameter copper tubing cut to the following lengths:

~ 3 inches (7.5 cm), 4 inches (10 cm), 5 inches (12.5 cm), 6 inches (15 cm), 7 inches (17.5 cm), 8 inches (20 cm), 9 inches (22.5 cm), and 10 inches (25 cm)

~ 8 pieces of string, each 6 inches (15 cm) long

~ electrical tape

~ broomstick or thin pole

~ 2 chairs

~ chopstick, drumstick, or wooden pencil

~ copper tubing of different diameters, of the same lengths as those listed above (optional)

WHAT YOU DO

1. Arrange the pieces of copper tubing in order of length from shortest to longest.

2. On each piece of the tubing, use electrical tape to secure 1 inch (2.5 cm) of the string to one side of the end. Tape 1 inch (2.5 cm) of the other end of the string to the opposite side of the pipe, so that the string forms a loop. With tape, wrap the area of each pipe where the string is attached to ensure the string is firmly in place.

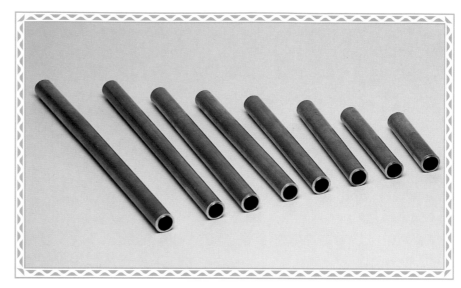

Your pieces of copper tubing should hang on the string in this order.

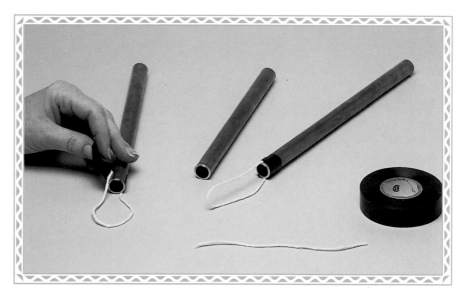

The chime on the right is properly fitted and ready to hang.

6. If you're also using the optional pieces of copper tubing listed above, compare the sound of two copper tubes that are of different widths but equal length. Do they sound the same?

WHAT HAPPENED?

Each of the pipes made a different sound when you struck or "played" it with the chopstick. The striking action caused the copper pipe to vibrate. The longer pipes made a deeper-pitched sound and the shorter pipes made a higher-pitched sound. Because the pipes are suspended by string, they are able to vibrate freely and the note is played for quite a long time before it stops. The air inside each of the copper tubes also vibrates, which makes the notes louder than if you had used solid copper bars.

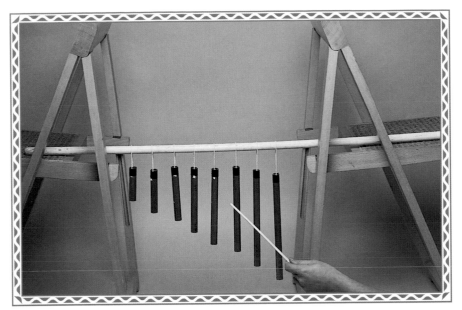
Correctly assembled chimes.

3. Slide the end of the broom handle or pole through each of the string loops with the pipes arranged in order from shortest to longest.
4. Position the two chairs a little ways apart, and place each end of the broom or pole on a chair so the strung pipes can swing freely. Arrange the pipes along the pole so that they are about 3 inches (7.5 cm) apart.
5. Use the chopstick to hit each of the pipes. Can you play a tune?

"ROCK" MUSIC

The Earth has its very own built-in bells. In some places, boulders and rocks ring when they are struck with hammers, and are sometimes called "ringing rocks." Scientists who have studied these "musical" rocks believe that the reason the rocks sound like bells is because the insides of the rocks are under intense pressure. Even small bits of rock chipped off from the boulders ring with the same tone. If the rocks are moved, suspended, or even clamped, they still produce a beautiful tone.

Rimshot

When you look at or play a drum it seems like a pretty simple instrument, especially when you compare it to a piano, flute, or a violin. No matter where you hit the drum, it makes a noise. However, the way a drum works to make different sounds is actually quite complicated. Where you hit the drum's surface is very important. To make a drum, a thin membrane such as an animal hide or a strong plastic like fiberglass is stretched over a circular frame. This membrane and frame form the drumhead—the part of the drum you touch with your hands or a drumstick to make music. Some drums have two heads—one on the top and one on the bottom of the drum. Both these heads must be tuned so they vibrate in sympathy with the drum. Some drums have only one head, with a hollow space below the head that causes resonance, so these drums give a deeper sound when they are played. Drums give percussive rhythm or beat

and accent to the other instruments they accompany. This is why a drum sound never clashes with the rest of the band. Here's a way to create a big noise and learn some science at the same time.

WHAT YOU NEED

- large metal bowl
- thick plastic disposable garbage bag
- felt-tipped marker
- ruler
- scissors
- helper
- masking tape
- penny
- chopstick (optional)

WHAT YOU DO

1. Place the bowl upside down on the plastic bag. Use the felt marker to trace a line around the bowl on the bag where the two meet.

2. Use the ruler to measure 4 inches (10 cm) out from the line at a few points and connect these marks to draw another circle on the bag. Cut along the larger circle with the scissors.

3. Have your helper pull on the ends of the plastic, keeping the plastic taut, as you fold the plastic against the side of the bowl and secure it using long strips of masking tape. This is your drum, and the top surface is the drumhead.

4. When the plastic is securely in place, turn the bowl over so that it is right side up. Check the tension of the drumhead by bouncing a penny on the surface of the plastic. The penny should

bounce when you drop it on the drumhead. If your drumhead isn't tight enough, adjust it by pulling the plastic down tighter on the sides of the bowl and attaching it with more tape.

5. Use your hand or the chopstick to play a beat.

WHAT HAPPENED?

You made a drum. Your bowl drum most resembles a tympani drum, also known as a "kettle drum." In an orchestra, these drums are located at the very back of the setup, behind all the other instruments. These huge drums have a large, nearly enclosed air mass held inside the copper kettles below the membrane. When the head or membrane is struck, the air moves around inside the kettle and as a result the frequencies are changed. Percussionists, or people who play drums, tune these huge instruments in two ways—by turning special tension rods that are used for this purpose, and sometimes by using a pedal device that

changes the pitch. Drummers know that when you hit the drumhead in its center, it makes a dead sound, but when you hit it off center, it makes a more lively sound. Drummers call the center of the drum the "dead center." If you get the chance, watch a tympani player in a symphony. Do these percussionists usually hit their drums off center? "Rimshot" is a term used by drummers to describe a method of playing a drum. The drummer hits the topside rim of the drum with a stick at the same time as he or she hits the drumhead. This produces a very loud sound, or accent, on the drum.

Rainsticks

No one knows what sound a light saber makes, because there's no such thing as a light saber. People who make movies have to be very inventive to create special effects sounds. Sometimes they take sounds made with everyday materials and use hi-tech computer programs to turn them into out-of-this-world noises. Or they might shake boxes filled with shards of glass to simulate walking on broken glass, or twist thin sheets of metal to create a sound like thunder. With this experiment, you can create your own special effect and make it "rain" indoors.

WHAT YOU NEED

- ⬳ long cardboard mailing tube about 2 inches (5 cm) in diameter, with plastic caps for ends

- ⬳ colored electrical or duct tape

- ⬳ adult helper

- ⬳ hammer

- ⬳ about thirty 1¾-inch (4.5-cm) nails

- ⬳ ½ cup (125 ml) unpopped popcorn or very small pebbles

WHAT YOU DO

1. Fit one of the plastic caps firmly in one end of the cardboard tube. Use the tape to very firmly secure this end. It will be really messy if this falls off while you are making this instrument.

2. Have your adult helper hammer the nails into the sides of the tube in several different places from the top to the bottom of the tube. The tips of the nails should all be inside the tube.

3. Pour the popcorn or pebbles into the tube, then seal the open end of the tube with the remaining plastic cap. As you did with the cap on the other end, tape the cap firmly in place.

4. Have your adult helper wrap the electrical or duct tape around the tube so that the entire cardboard surface is covered. This keeps the nails in place and can be used to give your rainstick an interesting and colorful design.

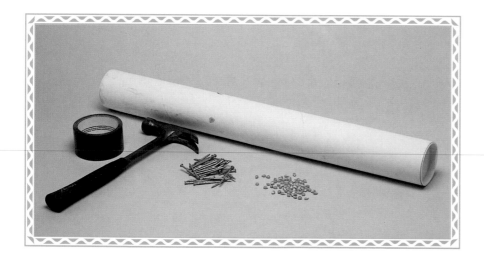

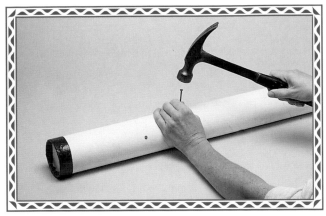

An adult should do all steps that involve a hammer and nail, like this one.

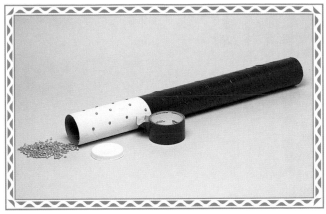

When the rainstick is almost completed, pour in the corn and secure the second cap with tape.

5. Turn the rainstick over so that the popcorn or pebbles fall inside it. Listen to the falling "rain."

WHAT HAPPENED?

As the popcorn or pebbles hit each nail, they produced a tinkling noise that sounded like rain. As the small objects hit the nails, they caused the nails to vibrate. This combination of vibrating nails and small "pinging" sounds from the popcorn or pebbles sounded like rain falling.

"Canned" Music

Musicians who play wind instruments such as the flute blow across an opening in the instrument to produce a beautiful high-pitched sound. As the musician blows, air enters the tube and causes the air inside the flute to vibrate. The length of the tube is changed by the player's covering up different holes in the side of the tube. When a longer column of air vibrates, a deeper sound is produced; a shorter column gives a higher-pitched sound. Here is a way to try making your own upright glass "flutes."

WHAT YOU NEED

~~ 5 bottles the same size and shape

~~ 5 bottles of different sizes and shapes

~~ water

~~ measuring cup

WHAT YOU DO

1. Fill the five same-sized bottles with various amounts of water. Fill one nearly all the way with water, and one with just a little bit of water. Line the bottles up according to the amounts of water in the bottle from the one with the least volume to the one with the greatest volume.

2. Create a noise by blowing across the mouth of each bottle. What sound does each of the bottles make?

3. Fill each of the different-sized bottles to the top with water. Next, pour ½ cup of water from each bottle. Line the bottles up and blow across the mouths of the bottles. How does this sound compare to the sound made by the identical bottles?

Same-sized bottles with different amounts of water.

Different-sized bottles with identical amounts of water.

WHAT HAPPENED?

As you blew across the water-filled bottles, you heard a sound. You created sounds of different pitches in the bottles in step 1. The more air the bottle contained, the lower the pitch of its sound was. When you changed the shape of the bottle, but kept the air volume the same in step 3, the frequencies were almost identical and the sounds had the same pitch.

Reed My Lips

Musical instruments such as clarinets and oboes don't create music the same way as a flute or a piccolo. Inside the mouthpiece of these instruments is something called a **reed**. When you blow into the mouthpiece, you make the reed vibrate. This causes the air inside the pipe to begin to vibrate. The noise then comes out the fat, cone-shaped end of the instrument called the flare. (Here's a way to clean up your garden and make beautiful music at the same time.

WHAT YOU NEED

➤ long, fat reed or blade of grass from the garden

➤ soap and water

WHAT YOU DO

1. Find several long, fat reeds and wash them off to make sure they have no pesticides or other nasty things, like dirt or bugs, on them.

2. Hold the reed between your thumbs, so that it falls between the place created by your knuckle and the side of your hand.

3. Purse your lips together, place your mouth against the reed, and blow really hard. You may have to adjust the position of the reed to get the right sound.

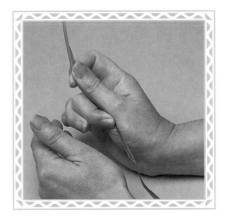

4. When you can successfully blow a loud noise, rotate your thumbs inward and outward as you blow onto the reed. How did this change the sound?

WHAT HAPPENED?

When you blew through your thumbs, your breath caused the reed to vibrate back and forth.

You could change the pitch of the sound by varying the amount of space between your thumbs. When a person who plays a clarinet wants to produce a certain note, the musician chooses the fingering, adjusts the pressure of his or her lips against the reed, then blows. The soft, springy reed then vibrates at the correct frequency for the note to be played. The clarinet player doesn't have to make the reed vibrate at the correct frequency; the airflow in the tube alters the vibration so that it is exactly right. This is called positive feedback. This results in the ability to play a note that lasts a long, or sustained, time.

The kind of feedback with which most people are familiar is an acoustical feedback from a loudspeaker. This is when a terrible howl or screech comes from a microphone, usually in an auditorium. Feedback such as this is caused when the sound from a loudspeaker comes back to the microphone in phase with a signal that is already there. The sound will continue to build up and make that terrible noise. Feedback can ruin electronic components, especially the coils in speakers.

Glossary

acoustics: the branch of science dealing with sound; the sound qualities of a room or hall.
antinode: the area between nodes where the greatest movement occurs.
antinoise: sound waves generated at specific frequencies to dampen or eliminate background sound
auditory canal: the tube-like section of the outer ear
auditory nerve: the nerve that sends messages from the cochlea to the brain.
beat: to hit something repeatedly; to mark time by tapping; to combine two sound waves of different frequencies to create an additional sound of a different frequency; a unit of time in music.
bel (B): unit for expressing the intensity of sound.
binaural hearing: hearing with both ears.

chromatic scale: a musical scale consisting of all twelve notes a semitone apart in one octave.
cochlea: the small, snail-shaped organ of the inner ear.
consonance: a pleasant or harmonious combination of musical sounds.
decibel (dB): one tenth of a bel.
diaphragm: the muscular layer between the chest and abdominal cavities of the body; a thin membrane that vibrates in response to sound to make an electrical signal in a microphone or that is vibrated to make a sound as in a loudspeaker.
dissonance: an inharmonious combination of sounds.
Doppler effect: the apparent change in frequency of sound or light waves caused by the difference in the speed of the source and the observer.

echo: the repetition of a sound after it is reflected off of a surface.
echolocation: a means of detecting objects by sending out sounds that are reflected back to the observer.
energy: the ability to cause objects to move.
epiglottis: the valve-like piece of tissue at the back of the throat that closes when food is eaten to keep food out of the airway.
fifth: the interval between the first and fifth notes on a scale
five-tone pentatonic scale: a musical scale based on intervals of a fifth.
fourth: the interval between the first and fourth notes on a scale.
frequency: the number of vibrations or waves in a given period of time.
fundamental: the lowest frequency of each note that an instrument can produce.

harmonics: any of the pure tones making up a complex musical sound, including the fundamental and all of the overtones.

hertz: the international unit for frequency; one hertz (Hz) is one cycle per second.

incus, or anvil bone: a small bone in the middle ear between the malleus and the stapes.

infrasound: sound with a frequency less than that which can be detected by the human ear.

inner ear: the innermost section of the ear, containing the cochlea and the semi-circular canals.

intensity: the amount of energy per unit of space.

larynx, or voice box: the part of the body most responsible for voice; it contains the vocal cords.

longitudinal wave: waves running lengthwise, as opposed to transverse waves.

Mach 1: a number representing the ratio of the speed of an object to the speed of sound.

malleus, or hammer bone: a small bone in the middle ear touching the eardrum and the incus.

membrane: a thin, soft flexible sheet of material or tissue.

middle ear: the middle section of the ear, containing the eardrum and the three ear bones.

molecule: a small particle consisting of two or more atoms.

monochord: a musical instrument made with a single string and a moveable bridge.

node: the point, line, or surface of a vibrating object that is not moving.

noise: a discordant or unpleasant sound.

notation: the system of symbols used in music.

octave: the interval between the first and eighth notes on a scale.

oscillator: an electronic device that generates pure notes, or notes at a single frequency.

oscilloscope: a device that displays a wave or curve like signal made from a rapidly changing electrical signal.

outer ear: the outermost section of the ear including the pinna and the auditory canal.

pinna: the funnel-shaped section of the outer ear.

pitch: the quality of sound determined by the frequency of sound waves when they reach the ear; a high frequency sound will have a high pitch.

region of rarefaction: the region in a fluid where molecules are spaced further apart when a sound wave passes through.

region of compression: the region in a fluid where molecules are pushed closer together when a sound wave passes through.

resonance: the production of or increase in a sound when exposed to another sound at the same frequency.

scale: a series of musical tones arranged in order of rising or falling pitch.

semicircular canals: fluid-filled tubes in the inner ear, used for balance.

semitone (S): the notes played by adjacent keys on the piano; an octave is divided into twelve equal semitones.

sonar: a device which gives off high-frequency sound waves underwater and registers the reflected sound waves as they bounce off of underwater objects.

sound: vibrations in air or water that stimulate the auditory nerve and produce the sensation of hearing.

sound effects: sounds produced artificially or recorded to use in the sound tracks of movies, plays, radio or television.

standing wave: a wave created when two waves moving in opposite directions combine, with nodes and antinodes in fixed positions.

stapes, or stirrup bone: the small bone in the middle ear between the incus and the cochlea.

stereo: sounds using two speakers playing different sounds to give a blend of sounds.

synesthesia: a condition that causes some people to perceive sounds as a colors.

timbre: the quality of sound that allows an observer to tell the difference between different musical instruments; timbre is determined by the harmonics of the sound.

tone (T): an interval of two semitones; a distinct and identifiable musical or vocal sound.

transverse wave: a wave which goes from side to side, as opposed to a longitudinal wave.

tympanic membrane or eardrum: the thin membrane of the middle ear that vibrates when a sound is heard.

ultrasound: sound with a frequency greater than that which can be detected by the human ear.

vacuum: a completely empty space.

vibration: a movement back and forth.

vocal cords: two pairs of membrane-like cords in the larynx.

wave: a series of vibrations that moves outwards from a source.

wavelength: the distance between identical points on two adjacent waves.

white noise: a sound containing all of the audible frequencies distributed evenly.

Index

acoustics, 25

animals, hearing range of, 16

balance, keeping, and the inner ear, 35–36

Bell, Alexander, 39

bells/chimes, 69
  how they produce music, 71
  how to make your own, 70–71

bow for stringed instruments, importance of its sticky coating, 67–68

carsick. See balance, keeping, and the inner ear

chimes. See bells/chimes

decibels, 39

determining the direction sound is coming from, 32–33, 33–34

dissonance, 60

Doppler effect, 21–22

Doppler, Dr. Christian Johann, 21

drums, 59, 62
  how they produce sound, 72, 73
  how to make your own, 73

ear, parts of the, 29

ears, how they work, 28, 30–31

experiment, connection between the inner ear and balance, 35–36

experiment, sounds from the mouth, 40–41

experiment, vocal cords, 42–43

experiments, hearing, 27–29, 30–31, 32–33, 33–34, 36–37, 38–39, 44–45

experiments, music, 47–48, 49–51, 51–53, 53–54, 55–56, 58–59, 60–61

experiments, musical instrument, 63–64, 65–67, 67–68, 69–71, 72–73, 74–75, 75–76, 77–78

experiments, sound, 9–10, 11–12, 13–14, 15–16, 17–18, 19–20, 21–22, 22–23, 24–25

flute, 58, 59, 62
  how it produces music, 75
  how to make your own upright glass flutes, 76

frequency, fundamental, 51–53, 55, 56, 58

guitar, 56, 62, 67
  how it produces music, 63–64
  tuning strings of the, 65

harmonics, 52–53, 58, 59

hearing, 26–45
  and aging, 38–39
  exaggeration of, 28, 36–37
  experiments (see experiments, hearing)
  process of, 28
  your own voice, 44–45

hearing, binaural, 33

Hertz, Heinrich, 15

infrasound, 18

instruments, musical, 56, 58, 59, 62–78. See also specific instruments; instruments, reed; instruments, stringed

instruments, reed

how they produce music, 77
  how to make your own, 77–78

instruments, stringed, 62, 63, 65, 68. See also guitar, violin

making sounds from the mouth, process of, 41

materials for experiments, 7

monochord, making your own, 49–50

music, 46–61, 62–73, 75–78
  and mathematics, 4, 49–51
  experiments (see experiments, music; experiments, musical instrument)
  vs. noise, 46, 60–61

notation, music, 57

oscillator, 18

oscilloscope, 16

parents, note to, 5–6

piano, 55, 56, 58, 60, 62, 68

pitch, 17–18, 21, 22, 38, 39, 42, 43, 47, 48, 52, 54, 58, 64, 65, 73, 75, 76, 78

Pythagoras, 49, 50, 51

rain, simulating, with rainsticks, 74–75

recognizing a recording of your own voice, 44–45

resonance, 55–56

safety in performing experiments, 6–7

scale, chromatic, 51, 54

scales, musical, 54

seasick. See balance, keeping, and the inner ear

singing/singers, 47–48, 55, 63

sonic booms, 37

sound
  and color, 26–27
  creation of, 9–10
  definition of, 8
  echoes, 22–23
  experiments (see experiments, sound)
  frequencies, 15–16, 17, 18, 21, 22, 48, 51, 52
  intensity, 39
  measurement of, 15–16
  muffling of, 24–25
  physics of, 8–25
  speed of, 20
  traveling of, 13–14, 19–20
  waves, 8, 11–12, 13–14, 15–16, 20, 22, 23, 46, 50, 52, 53, 54, 61, 67

sound, stereo, 32–33

sounds from the mouth, influences on, 40–41, 42–43

sounds, whale, 43

Stradivari, Antonio, 59

Stradivarius violin, 59, 67

teachers, note to, 5–6

timbre, 58–59

Torres, Antonio de, 63

Tyndall, John, 13

ultrasound, 18

violin, 58, 59, 68
  how it produces music, 67
  importance of the wood it is made from, 65, 67

vocal cords, 43

waves. See also sound, waves
  longitudinal, 12
  standing, 53–54
  transverse, 12

white noise vs. antinoise, 61